Fodor's P O C

D1458988

santa fe
& taos

Excerpted from *Fodor's New Mexico*

fodor's travel publications
new york • toronto • london • sydney • auckland

www.fodors.com

contents

maps

ON THE ROAD WITH FODOR'S

EVERY TRIP IS A SIGNIFICANT TRIP. Acutely aware of that fact, we've pulled out all the stops in preparing Fodor's *Pocket Santa Fe & Taos*. And to direct you to the places that are truly worth your time and money, we've rallied the team of endearingly picky know-it-alls we're pleased to call our writers. Having seen all corners of Santa Fe and Taos, they're real experts. If you knew them, you'd poll them for tips yourself.

Jeanie Puleston Fleming is an avid hiker and skier in the mountains of northern New Mexico, where she has lived for the past 20 years. She writes about the Southwest for national and regional publications.

A veritable font of practical information about the entire state, **Marilyn Haddrill** was the perfect updater for the Practical Information chapter. Marilyn has coauthored two suspense novels and writes for various publications, including *Final Frontier* and the *Dallas Morning News*.

Kathleen McCloud, a visual artist and arts writer for local and national publications, has lived in the Santa Fe area for 12 years. Her expertise is in the traditional arts of the Southwest, particularly textile arts, as well as contemporary art. Her knowledge and appreciation of Southwestern architecture comes after many years of living with a house designer/builder, and hands-on experience building three houses in northern New Mexico.

Don't Forget to Write

Keeping a travel guide fresh and up-to-date is a big job. So we love your feedback—positive and negative—and follow up on all suggestions. Contact the New Mexico editor at editors@fodors. com or c/o Fodor's, 280 Park Avenue, New York, New York 10017. And have a wonderful trip!

Karen Cure

Karen Cure

Editorial Director

new mexico

UTAH
UTE MOUNTAIN INDIAN RES.
SOUTHERN UTE INDIAN RES
COLORADO
San Juan R.
Shiprock
Aztec
Farmington
Bloomfield
CARSON NAT'L FOR.
Dulce
Chama
APACHE INDIAN RES.
CARSON NAT'L FOR.
ROCKY MOUNTAINS
NAVAJO INDIAN RES.
ARIZONA
De-Na-Zin Wilderness
Bisti Wilderness
Nageezi
Chaco R.
SANTA FE NAT'L FOR.
Abiquiú
Rio Grande
Naschitti
Chaco Culture Nat'l Historic Park
Cuba
Española
Chimayó
Tohatchi
Los Alamos
Jemez Springs
BANDELIER NAT'L MON.
Crownpoint
Santa Fe
Gallup
Thoreau
CIBOLA NAT'L FOR.
Rio Puerco
Madrid
Bernalillo
Golden
Grants
Rio Rancho
Albuquerque
Zuñi
ZUÑI INDIAN RES.
LAGUNA INDIAN RES.
Tijeras
Moriarty
RAMAH NAVAJO RES.
El Malpais Nat'l Mon.
ACOMA INDIAN RES.
ISLETA INDIAN RES.
Las Lunas
Estancia
Fence Lake
Belen
Willard
Mountainair
Trechado
Quemado
Pie Town
Datil
Magdalena
Polvadera
Socorro
APACHE NAT'L FOR.
Bosque del Apache Nat'l Wildlife Refuge
Carrizozo
LINCOLN NAT'L FOR.
Mogollon
Glenwood
Winston
Chloride
Elephant Butte Lake S.P.
Elephant Butte Lake
WHITE SANDS MISSILE RANGE
Three Rivers
Ruidoso
Mescalero
Tularosa
GILA NAT'L FOR.
Truth or Consequences
Caballo Lake S.P.
Cloudcroft
Alamogordo
Pinos Altos
Kingston
Lake Valley
Gila R.
San Andreas Nat'l Wildlife Refuge
WHITE SANDS NAT'L MON.
Redrock
Silver City
Bayard
Hatch
LINCOLN NAT'L FOR.
Cooke's Peak
Nutt
Radium Springs
Organ
Lordsburg
Las Cruces
Mesilla
Deming
N
0
50 miles
75 km
San Miguel
Anthony
Hachita
Columbus
El Paso
MEXICO
Ciudad Juárez

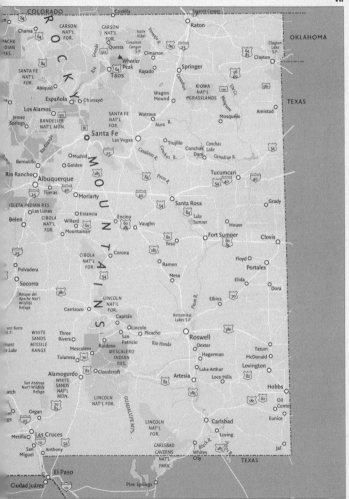

santa fe
& taos

In This Chapter

introducing santa fe and taos

NEW MEXICO'S TAGLINE is more than a marketing cliché. The state is truly a "Land of Enchantment," and Santa Fe is indisputably "the City Different." Surrounded by mind-expanding mountain views and filled with sinuous streets that discourage car traffic but invite leisurely exploration, Santa Fe welcomes visitors with characteristic warmth, if not some trepidation. Rapid growth and development have taken their toll, prompting many local residents to worry about becoming too much like "everywhere else," and you'll hear various complaints about encroaching commercialism and its attendant T-shirt shops and fast-food restaurants that interfere with the rhythms of life here.

But despite (or perhaps, occasionally, because of) a surfeit of trendy restaurants, galleries, and boutiques that tout regional fare and wares, both authentic and artificial, Santa Fe remains a special place to visit. Commercialism notwithstanding, its deeply spiritual aura affects even nonreligious types in surprising ways, inspiring a reverence probably not unlike that which inspired the Spanish monks to name it the "City of Holy Faith." (Its full name is La Villa Real de la Santa Fe de San Francisco de Asís, or the Royal City of the Holy Faith of St. Francis of Assisi.) A kind of mystical Catholicism blended with ancient Native American lore and beliefs flourishes throughout northern New Mexico in tiny mountain villages that have seen little change through the centuries. Tales of miracles, spontaneous healings, and spiritual visitations thrive in the old adobe churches that line the High Road that leads north of Santa Fe to Taos.

If Santa Fe is spiritual, sophisticated, and occasionally superficial, Taos, 65 mi away, is very much an outpost despite its relative proximity to the capital. Compared with Santa Fe, Taos is smaller, feistier, quirkier, tougher, and very independent. Taoseños are a study in contradictions: Wary of strangers and suspicious of outsiders, they nevertheless accept visitors with genuine warmth and pride. Rustic and delightfully unpretentious, the town contains a handful of upscale restaurants with cuisines and wine lists as innovative as what you might find in New York. It's a haven for aging hippies, creative geniuses, cranky misanthropes, and anyone else who wants a good quality of life in a place that accepts new arrivals without a lot of questions—as long as they don't offend longtime residents with their city attitudes.

Unifying these towns and the terrain around them is the appeal of the land and the people. It's the character of the residents and their attitude toward the land that imbue New Mexico with its enchanted spirit. First-time visitors discover the unexpected pleasures of a place where time is measured not by linear calculations of hours, days, weeks, and years but in a circular sweep of crop cycles, gestation periods, the rotation of generations, and the changing of seasons.

NEW AND NOTEWORTHY

In a setback to New Mexico's environment, a controlled burn of the underbrush at Bandelier National Monument in May 2000 turned into a fierce wildfire. More than 200 homes were destroyed in **Los Alamos,** though Los Alamos National Laboratory did not suffer serious damage. At the same time, the state was suffering its worst drought in 30 years. Drenching rains later in the summer, however, helped much of the state's mountain and desert areas to begin recovering from dry conditions.

PLEASURES AND PASTIMES

DINING

New Mexico's cuisine is a delicious and extraordinary mixture of Pueblo, Spanish colonial, and Mexican and American frontier cooking. Recipes that came from Spain via Mexico were adapted for local ingredients—chiles, corn, pork, wild game, pinto beans, honey, apples, and piñon nuts—and have remained much the same ever since.

In Santa Fe and Taos, babies cut their teeth on fresh flour tortillas and quickly develop a taste for sopaipillas, deep-fried, puff-pastry pillows, drizzled with honey. But it is the chile pepper, whether red or green, that is the heart and soul of northern New Mexican cuisine. You might be a bit surprised to learn that ristras, those strings of bright red chiles that seem to hang everywhere, are sold more for eating here than for decoration. More varieties of chiles—upward of 90—are grown in New Mexico than anywhere else in the world.

In most restaurants you can dress as casually as you like. Those in the major business hotels tend to be a bit more formal, but as the evening wears down, so do the restrictions.

OUTDOOR ACTIVITIES AND SPORTS
Canoeing and River Rafting

You can challenge yourself on New Mexico's rivers. The Taos Box, a 17-mi run through the churning rapids of the Rio Grande, is one of America's most exciting rafting experiences.

Golf

With several dozen courses, the state has a respectable share of turf, and the dry climate makes playing very comfortable. There are excellent public courses in Santa Fe and Taos.

Horse Racing

Horse racing with pari-mutuel betting is very popular in New Mexico. One of the more favored of the state's tracks is Downs at Santa Fe, 5 mi south of town.

Skiing

New Mexico contains many world-class downhill ski areas. Snowmaking equipment is used in most areas to ensure a long season, usually from Thanksgiving through Easter. The Santa Fe Ski Area averages 250 inches of dry-powder snow a year; it accommodates all levels of skiers on more than 40 trails. Within a 90-mi radius of Taos are resorts with slopes for all levels of skiers, as well as snowmobile and cross-country ski trails. The Taos Ski Valley resort is recognized internationally for its challenging terrain and European-style ambience.

PARKS AND MONUMENTS

New Mexico's state park network includes nearly four dozen parks, ranging from high-mountain lakes and pine forests in the north to the Chihuahuan Desert lowlands of the south. Parks and monuments close to Santa Fe include Pecos National Historic Park and Jemez State Monument. The Carson National Forest is near Taos.

RESERVATIONS AND PUEBLOS

New Mexico's Pueblo cultures, each with its own reservation and distinct but overlapping history, art, and customs, evolved out of the highly civilized Anasazi culture that built Chaco Canyon. Pueblos dating back centuries are located near Santa Fe and Taos; the best time to visit them is during one of their many year-round public dance ceremonies. Admission is free to pueblos unless otherwise indicated. Donations, however, are always welcome.

The pueblos around Santa Fe—San Ildefonso, Nambé, Pojoaque, and Santa Clara—are more infused with Spanish culture than are the pueblos in other areas. Dwellers here also have the keenest business sense when dealing with the sale of handicrafts and art and with matters touristic. The famous Taos Pueblo, unchanged through the centuries, is the personification of classic Pueblo Native American culture. It and the Picurís Pueblo near Taos have first-rate recreational facilities.

When visiting pueblos and reservations, you're expected to follow a certain etiquette. Each pueblo has its own regulations for the use of still and video cameras and video and tape recorders, as well as for sketching and painting. Some pueblos prohibit photography altogether. Others, such as Santa Clara, prohibit photography at certain times, such as during ritual dances. Still others allow photography but require a permit, which usually costs about $5 or $10 for a still camera. The privilege of setting up an easel and painting all day will cost you as little as $35 or as much as $150 (at Taos Pueblo). Be sure to ask permission before photographing anyone in the pueblos; it's also customary to give the subject a dollar or two for agreeing to be photographed. Native American law prevails on the pueblos, and violations of photography regulations could result in confiscation of cameras.

Specific restrictions for the various pueblos are noted in the individual descriptions. Other rules are described below.

● Possessing or using drugs and/or alcohol on Native American land is forbidden.

● Ritual dances often have serious religious significance and should be respected as such. Silence is mandatory—that means no questions about ceremonies or dances while they're being performed. Don't walk across the dance plaza during a performance, and don't applaud afterward.

- Kiva and ceremonial rooms are restricted to pueblo members only.

- Cemeteries are sacred. They're off-limits to all visitors and should never be photographed.

- Unless pueblo dwellings are clearly marked as shops, don't wander or peek inside. Remember, these are private homes.

- Many of the pueblo buildings are hundreds of years old. Don't try to scale adobe walls or climb on top of buildings, or you may come tumbling down.

- Don't litter. Nature is sacred on the pueblos, and defacing land can be a serious offense.

SHOPPING
Antiques

You'll find everything in New Mexico's shops, from early Mexican typewriters to period saddles, ceramic pots, farm tools, pioneer aviation equipment, and yellowed newspaper clippings about Kit Carson and D. H. Lawrence.

Art

Santa Fe, with more than 150 galleries, is the arts capital of the Southwest and a leading arts center nationally. Taos is not far behind. Native American art, Western art, Hispanic art, contemporary art, sculpture, photography, prints, ceramics, jewelry, folk art, junk art—it's all for sale in New Mexico, produced by artists of international and local renown.

Crafts

Hispanic handcrafted furniture and *santos* (saints) command high prices from collectors. Santos are religious carvings and paintings in the form of *bultos* (three-dimensional carvings) and *retablos* (holy images painted on wood or tin). Colorful handwoven Hispanic textiles, tinwork, ironwork, and straw appliqué are also in demand. Native American textiles, rugs, kachina dolls, baskets, silver jewelry, turquoise, pottery, beadwork, ornamental shields, drums, and ceramics can be found almost everywhere. Prices range from thousands of dollars for a rare 1930s kachina doll to a few cents for hand-wrapped bundles of sage, juniper, sweet grass, and lavender that are used by Native Americans in healing ceremonies, gatherings, and daily cleansing of the home.

Spices

Roadside stands sell chile ristras, and shops all over the state carry chile powder and other spices. You'll catch the smell of chile peppers from the road; walk in a store and your eyes may water and your mouth salivate. For many, especially natives of the Southwest, *picante* is the purest, finest word in the Spanish language. It means hot—spicy hot. All around you, in boxes, bags, packets, jars, and cans, there's everything picante—salsas, chile pastes, powders, herbs, spices, peppers, barbecue sauce, and fiery potions in bottles.

In This Chapter

Updated by Kathleen McCloud

santa fe

WITH ITS CRISP, CLEAN AIR AND BRIGHT, SUNNY WEATHER, Santa Fe couldn't be more welcoming. On a plateau at the base of the Sangre de Cristo Mountains—at an elevation of 7,000 ft—the city is surrounded by remnants of a 2,000-year-old Pueblo civilization and filled with reminders of almost four centuries of Spanish and Mexican rule. The town's placid central Plaza, which dates from the early 17th century, has been the site of bullfights, public floggings, gunfights, battles, political rallies, promenades, and public markets over the years. A uniquely appealing destination, Santa Fe is fabled for its rows of chic art galleries, superb restaurants, and shops selling Southwestern furnishings and cowboy gear.

La Villa Real de la Santa Fe de San Francisco de Asís (the Royal City of the Holy Faith of St. Francis of Assisi) was founded in the early 1600s by Don Pedro de Peralta, who planted his banner in the name of Spain. In 1680 the region's Pueblo people rose in revolt, burning homes and churches and killing hundreds of Spaniards. After an extended siege in Santa Fe, the Spanish colonists were driven out of New Mexico. The tide turned 12 years later, when General Don Diego de Vargas returned with a new army from El Paso and recaptured Santa Fe.

To commemorate de Vargas's victory, Las Fiestas de Santa Fe have been held every year since 1712. The nation's oldest community celebration takes place on the weekend after Labor Day, with parades, mariachi bands, pageants, the burning of *Zozóbra*—also known as Old Man Gloom—and nonstop parties. "Fiesta" (as it's referred to locally) is but one of many annual opportunities for revelry—from the arrival of the rodeo and the opening week of the Santa Fe Opera in summer to traditional Pueblo dances at Christmastime.

Following de Vargas's defeat of the Pueblos, the then-grand Camino Real (Royal Road), stretching from Mexico City to Santa Fe, brought an army of conquistadors, clergymen, and settlers to the northernmost reaches of Spain's New World conquests. In 1820 the Santa Fe Trail—a prime artery of U.S. westward expansion—spilled a flood of covered wagons from Missouri onto the Plaza. A booming trade with the United States was born. After Mexico achieved independence from Spain in 1821, its subsequent rule of New Mexico further increased this commerce.

The Santa Fe Trail's heyday ended with the arrival of the Atchison, Topeka & Santa Fe Railway in 1880. The trains, and later the nation's first highways, brought a new type of settler to Santa Fe—artists who fell in love with its cultural diversity, history, and magical color and light. Their presence attracted tourists, who quickly became a primary source of income for the largely poor populace.

Santa Fe is renowned for its arts, tricultural (Native American, Hispanic, and Anglo) heritage, and adobe architecture. The Pueblo people introduced adobe to the Spanish, who in turn developed the adobe brick style of construction. In a relatively dry, treeless region, adobe was a suitable natural building material. Melding into the landscape with their earthen colors and rounded, flowing lines, the pueblos and villages were hard to see from afar and thus somewhat camouflaged from raiding nomadic tribes. The region's distinctive architecture no longer repels visitors, it attracts them.

Among the smallest state capitals in the country, Santa Fe has no major airport (Albuquerque's is the nearest). The city's population, an estimated 70,000, swells to nearly double that figure in summer. In winter the skiers arrive, lured by the challenging slopes of Ski Santa Fe and Taos Ski Valley. Geared for tourists, Santa Fe can put a serious dent in your travel budget. Prices are highest in June, July, and August. Between September and November and in April they're lower, and (except for the major holidays) from December to March they're the lowest.

HERE AND THERE

Humorist Will Rogers said on his first visit to Santa Fe, "Whoever designed this town did so while riding on a jackass, backwards, and drunk." The maze of narrow streets and alleyways confounds motorists, but with shops and restaurants, a flowered courtyard, or an eye-catching gallery at nearly every turn, they're a delight for pedestrians. The trickle of water called the Santa Fe River runs east, parallel to Alameda Street, from the Sangre de Cristos Mountains to the open prairie southwest of town, where it disappears into a narrow canyon before joining the Rio Grande. But in New Mexico there is a *dicho*, or old saying, "*agua es vida*"—"water is life"—be it ever so humble.

There are four state museums in Santa Fe, and purchasing a Museum of New Mexico pass is this most economic way to to visit them all. The four-day pass costs $10 and is sold at all of the four museums, which include the Palace of the Governors, Museum of Fine Arts, Museum of Indian Arts and Culture, and Museum of International Folk Art.

SANTA FE PLAZA

Much of the history of Santa Fe, New Mexico, the Southwest, and even the West has some association with Santa Fe's central Plaza, which New Mexico governor Don Pedro de Peralta laid out in 1607. The Plaza, already well established by the time of the Pueblo revolt in 1680, was the site of a bullring and of fiestas and fandangos. Freight wagons unloaded here after completing their arduous journey across the Santa Fe Trail. The American flag was raised over the Plaza in 1846, during the Mexican War, which resulted in Mexico's loss of all its territories in the present southwestern United States. For a time the Plaza was a tree-shaded park with a white picket fence. In the 1890s it was an expanse of lawn where uniformed bands played in an ornate gazebo. Particularly festive times on the Plaza are the weekend after Labor Day, during Las Fiestas de Santa Fe, and at Christmas, when all the trees are filled with lights and rooftops are outlined with *farolitos*, votive candles lit within paper-bag lanterns.

Numbers in the margin correspond to numbers on the Exploring Santa Fe map.

Sights to See

❸ GEORGIA O'KEEFFE MUSEUM. One of many East Coast artists who visited New Mexico in the first half of the 20th century, O'Keeffe fell in love with the region and returned to live and paint here, eventually emerging as the demigoddess of Southwestern art. This private museum devoted to the works of this Modernist painter opened in 1997. O'Keeffe's innovative view of the landscape is captured in *From the Plains*, inspired by her memory of the Texas plains, and *Jimson Weed*, a quintessential O'Keeffe study of one of her favorite plants. Special exhibitions with O'Keeffe's modernist peers are on view throughout the year. *217 Johnson St., tel. 505/995–0785. $5, free Fri. 5–8 PM. July–Oct., Tues.–Sun. 10–5, (extended hrs Wed. and Fri. 'til 8); Nov.–June, Tues., Thurs.–Sun. 10–5, (extended hrs Fri. 'til 8). www.okeeffemuseum.org*

❹ LA FONDA. A Santa Fe landmark, La Fonda (☞ Where to Stay, *below*) faces the southeast corner of the Plaza. A *fonda* (inn) has stood on this site for centuries. Architect Isaac Hamilton Rapp, whose Rio Grande–Pueblo Revival structures put Santa Fe style on the map, built this hotel in 1922. The hotel was remodeled in

1926 by another luminary of Santa Fe architecture, John Gaw Meem. The hotel was sold to the Santa Fe Railway in 1926 and became one of Fred Harvey's Harvey House hotels until 1968. Because of its proximity to the Plaza and its history as a gathering place for cowboys, trappers, traders, soldiers, frontier politicians, movie stars (Errol Flynn stayed here), artists, and writers, it is referred to as "The Inn at the End of the Trail." Major social events still take place here. *E. San Francisco St. at Old Santa Fe Trail, tel. 505/982–5511.*

★ ❷ **MUSEUM OF FINE ARTS.** Designed by Isaac Hamilton Rapp in 1917, the museum contains one of America's finest regional collections. It's also one of Santa Fe's earliest Pueblo Revival structures, inspired by the adobe structures at Acoma Pueblo. Split cedar *latillas* (branches set in a crosshatch pattern) and hand-hewn vigas make up the ceilings. The 8,000-piece permanent collection emphasizes the work of regional and nationally renowned artists, including the early Modernist Georgia O'Keeffe; realist Robert Henri; the "Cinco Pintores" (five painters) of Santa Fe (including Fremont Elis and Will Shuster); and members of the Taos Society of Artists (Ernest L. Blumenschein, Bert Geer Philips, Joseph Henry Sharp, and Eanger Irving Couse, among others). Many excellent examples of Spanish colonial–style furniture are on display. An interior *placita* (small plaza) with fountains, murals, and sculpture, and the St. Francis Auditorium are other highlights. Concerts and lectures are often held in the auditorium. *W. Palace Ave., tel. 505/476–5072. $5, 4-day pass $10, free Fri. 5–8 PM. Tues.–Thurs. and weekends 10–5, Fri. 10–8. www.nmculture.org*

❻ **MUSEUM OF THE INSTITUTE OF AMERICAN INDIAN ARTS.** Inside the handsomely renovated former post office, this museum contains the largest collection of contemporary Native American art in the United States. The paintings, photography, sculptures, prints, and traditional crafts exhibited here were created by past and present students and teachers. The institute itself, which moved to the College of Santa Fe campus, was founded as a one-

exploring santa fe

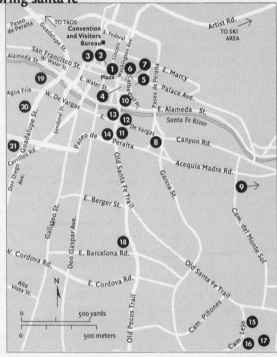

room studio classroom in the early 1930s by Dorothy Dunn, a beloved art teacher who played a critical role in launching the careers of many Native American artists. In the 1960s and 1970s it blossomed into the nation's premier center for Native American arts. Artist Fritz Scholder taught here for years, as did the sculptor Allan Houser. Among their disciples was the painter T. C. Cannon. *108 Cathedral Pl., tel. 505/988–6211 for events and parking information. $4. Daily 10–5.*

★ ✋ ❶ **PALACE OF THE GOVERNORS.** A humble-looking one-story adobe on the north side of the Plaza, the palace is the oldest public building in the United States. Built at the same time as the Plaza, circa 1607, it was the seat of four regional governments—those of Spain, Mexico, the Confederacy, and the U.S. territory that preceded New Mexico's statehood, which was achieved in 1912. The building was abandoned in 1680, following the Pueblo Revolt, but resumed its role as government headquarters when Don Diego de Vargas successfully returned in 1692. It served as the residence for 100 Spanish, Mexican, and American governors, including Governor Lew Wallace, who wrote his epic *Ben Hur* in its then drafty rooms, all the while complaining of the dust and mud that fell from its earthen ceiling.

The palace has been the central headquarters of the Museum of New Mexico since 1913 and houses the main section of the **State History Museum.** Permanent exhibits chronicle 450 years of New Mexico history, using maps, furniture, clothing, housewares, weaponry, and village models. With advance permission, students and researchers have access to the museum's extensive research library and its rare maps, manuscripts, and photographs (more than 120,000 prints and negatives). The palace is also home to the **Museum of New Mexico Press,** which prints books, pamphlets, and cards on antique presses and hosts bookbinding demonstrations, lectures, and slide shows. There is also an outstanding gift shop and bookstore. *Palace Ave., north side of the Plaza, tel. 505/476–5100. $5, 4-day pass $10 (good at all 4 state* museums in Santa Fe), free Fri. 5–8. Tues.–Thurs. and weekends 10–5, Fri. 10–8. www.palaceofthegovernors.org

Dozens of Native American vendors gather daily under the portal of the Palace of the Governors to display and sell pottery, jewelry, bread, and other goods. With few exceptions, the more than 500 artists and craftspeople registered to sell here are Pueblo or Navajo Indians. The merchandise for sale is required to meet Museum of New Mexico standards: all items are handmade or hand-strung in Native American households; silver jewelry is either sterling (92.5% pure) or coin (90% pure) silver; all metal jewelry bears the maker's mark, which is registered with the museum. Prices tend to reflect the high quality of the merchandise. Don't take photographs without permission.

★ **⑤ ST. FRANCIS CATHEDRAL.** This magnificent cathedral, a block east of the Plaza, is one of the rare significant departures from the city's ubiquitous pueblo architecture. Construction was begun in 1869 by Jean Baptiste Lamy, Santa Fe's first archbishop, working with French architects and Italian stonemasons. The Romanesque style was popular in Lamy's native home in the southwest of France. The circuit-riding cleric was sent by the Catholic Church to the Southwest to change the religious practices of its native population (to "civilize" them, as one period document puts it), and is buried in the crypt beneath the church's high altar. He was the inspiration behind Willa Cather's novel *Death Comes for the Archbishop* (1927).

A small adobe chapel on the northeast side of the cathedral, the remnant of an earlier church, embodies the Hispanic architectural influence so conspicuously absent from the cathedral itself. The chapel's *Nuestra Señora de la Paz* (Our Lady of Peace), popularly known as *La Conquistadora*, the oldest Madonna statue in the United States, accompanied Don Diego de Vargas on his reconquest of Santa Fe in 1692, a feat attributed to the statue's spiritual intervention. Every Friday the faithful adorn the statue with a new dress. Just south of the cathedral, where the parking lot meets Paseo de Peralta, is the **Archives of the Archdiocese Museum**, a small museum where many of the area's historic liturgical artifacts are on view. *231 Cathedral Pl., tel. 505/982–5619. Daily 8–5:45, except during mass. Mass celebrated Mon.–Sat. at 7 and 8:15 AM, 12:10 and 5:15 PM; Sun. at 6, 8, and 10 AM, noon, and 7 PM. Museum weekdays 9–4.*

➐ SENA PLAZA. Two-story buildings enclose this courtyard, which can be entered only through two small doorways on Palace Avenue. Surrounding the oasis of flowering fruit trees, a fountain, and inviting benches are unique, low-profile shops. The quiet courtyard is a good place for repose. The buildings, erected in the 1700s as a single-family residence, had quarters for blacksmiths, bakers, farmers, and all manner of help. *125 E. Palace Ave.*

CANYON ROAD

Once a Native American trail and an early 20th-century route for woodcutters and their burros, Canyon Road is now lined with art galleries, shops, and restaurants, earning it the nickname "the Art and Soul of Santa Fe." The narrow road begins at the eastern curve of Paseo de Peralta and stretches for about 2 mi at a slight incline toward the base of the mountains.

Most establishments are in authentic, old adobe homes with undulating thick walls that appear to have been carved out of the earth. Within many are contemporary and traditional works by artists from internationally renowned names like Fernando Botero to anonymous weavers of ancient Peruvian textiles.

There are few places as festive as Canyon Road on Christmas Eve, when thousands of *farolitos* (small lanterns) illuminate walkways, walls, roofs, and even trees. In May, the scent of lilacs wafts over the adobe walls, and in August, red hollyhocks enhance the surreal color of the blue sky on a dry summer day.

Sights to See

⑨ CRISTO REY CHURCH. Built in 1940 to commemorate the 400th anniversary of Francisco Vásquez de Coronado's exploration of the Southwest, this church is the largest Spanish adobe structure in the United States and is considered by many the finest example of Pueblo-style architecture anywhere. The church was constructed in the old-fashioned way by parishioners, who mixed the more than 200,000 mud-and-straw adobe bricks and hauled them into place. The 225-ton stone reredos (altar screen) is magnificent. *Canyon Rd. at Cristo Rey, where "Lower" Canyon Rd. becomes "Upper" Canyon Rd., tel. 505/983–8528. Daily 8–7.*

⑧ GERALD PETERS GALLERY. While under construction, this 32,000-square-ft building was dubbed the "ninth northern pueblo," its scale rivaling that of the eight northern pueblos around Santa Fe. The suavely designed Pueblo-style gallery is Santa Fe's premier showcase for American and European art from the 19th century to the present. It feels like a museum, but all the works are for sale. Pablo Picasso, Georgia O'Keeffe, Charles M. Russell, Deborah Butterfield, George Rickey, and members of the Taos Society are among the artists represented, along with nationally renowned contemporary artists. *1011 Paseo de Peralta, tel. 505/954–5700. Free. Mon.–Sat. 10–5.*

NEED A BREAK? — A good place to rest your feet is the **Backroom Coffeebar** (616 Canyon Rd., tel. 505/988–5323), which serves pastries and light snacks. Locals congregate in the courtyard or on the front portal of **Downtown Subscription** (376 Garcia St., tel. 505/983–3085), a block up from Paseo de Peralta and one block east of Canyon Road. You can pick up a paper here as well as coffee, light snacks, and pastries.

LOWER OLD SANTA FE TRAIL

It was along the Old Santa Fe Trail that wagon trains from Missouri rolled into town in the 1800s, forever changing Santa

Fe's destiny. This area off the Plaza is one of Santa Fe's most historic.

Sights to See

⑬ BARRIO DE ANALCO. Along the south bank of the Santa Fe River, the barrio—its name means "district on the other side of the water"—is one of America's oldest neighborhoods, settled in the early 1600s by the Tlaxcalan Indians (who were forbidden to live with the Spanish near the Plaza) and in the 1690s by soldiers who had helped recapture New Mexico after the Pueblo Revolt. Plaques on houses on East De Vargas Street will help you locate some of the important structures. Check the performance schedule at the **Santa Fe Community Theatre** on De Vargas Street, founded by writer Mary Austin and other Santa Feans in the 1920s.

⑩ LORETTO CHAPEL. A delicate Gothic church modeled after Sainte-Chapelle in Paris, Loretto was built in 1873 by the same French architects and Italian stonemasons who built St. Francis Cathedral. The chapel is known for the "Miraculous Staircase" that leads to the choir loft. Legend has it that the chapel was almost complete when it became obvious that there wasn't room to build a staircase to the choir loft. In answer to the prayers of the cathedral's nuns, an old bearded man arrived on a donkey, built a 20-ft staircase—using only a square, a saw, and a tub of water to season the wood—and then disappeared as quickly as he came. Many of the faithful believed it was St. Joseph himself. The staircase contains two complete 360-degree turns with no central support; no nails were used in its construction. The chapel closes for services and special events. Adjoining the chapel are a small museum and gift shop. *211 Old Santa Fe Trail, tel. 505/984–7971. $2. Mid-Oct.–mid-May, Mon.–Sat. 9–5, Sun. 10:30–5; mid-May–mid-Oct., Mon.–Sat. 8:30–6, Sun. 10:30–6.*

★ **⑭ NEW MEXICO STATE CAPITOL.** The symbol of the Zía Pueblo, which represents the Circle of Life, was the inspiration for the Capitol, also known as the Roundhouse. Doorways at opposing sides of this 1966 structure symbolize the four winds, the four directions, and the four seasons. Throughout the building are artworks from the outstanding collection of the Capitol Art Foundation, historical and cultural displays, and handcrafted furniture. The **Governor's Gallery** hosts temporary exhibits. Six acres of imaginatively landscaped gardens shelter outstanding sculptures. *Old Santa Fe Trail at Paseo de Peralta, tel. 505/986–4589. Free. Mon.–Sat. 8–5; tours at 10 and 2.*

⑫ THE OLDEST HOUSE. More than 800 years ago, Pueblo people built this structure out of "puddled" adobe (liquid mud poured between upright wooden frames). This house, which contains a gift shop, is said to be the oldest in the United States. *215 E. De Vargas St.*

★ **⑪ SAN MIGUEL MISSION.** The oldest church still in use in the United States, this simple earth-hued adobe structure was built in the early 17th century by the Tlaxcalan Indians of Mexico, who came to New Mexico as servants of the Spanish. Badly damaged in the 1680 Pueblo Revolt, the structure was restored and enlarged in 1710. On display in the chapel are priceless statues and paintings and the San José Bell, weighing nearly 800 pounds, which is believed to have been cast in Spain in 1356. In winter, the church sometimes closes before its official closing hour. Mass is held on Sunday at 5 PM. Next door in the back of the Territorial-style dormitories of the old St. Michael's High School, a **Visitor Information Center** distributes information on northern New Mexico. *401 Old Santa Fe Trail, tel. 505/983–3974. $1. Mission May– Oct., Mon.–Sat. 9–4:30, Sun. 3–4:30; Nov.–Apr., Mon–Sat. 10–4, Sun. 3–4:30. Information center weekdays 9–5.*

NEED A BREAK? Have a slice of pizza on the patio of **Upper Crust Pizza** (329 Old Santa Fe Trail, tel. 505/982–0000), next to the San Miguel Mission.

UPPER OLD SANTA FE TRAIL
Sights to See

★ **⑮ MUSEUM OF INDIAN ARTS AND CULTURE.** An interactive multimedia exhibition tells the story of Native American history in the Southwest, merging contemporary Native American experience with historical accounts and artifacts. The collection has some of New Mexico's oldest works of art: pottery vessels, fine stone and silver jewelry, intricate textiles, and other arts and crafts created by Pueblo, Navajo, and Apache artisans. You can also see art demonstrations and a video about the life and work of Pueblo potter Maria Martinez (☞ San Ildefonso Pueblo in Side Trips from Santa Fe). *710 Camino Lejo, tel. 505/476–1250. $5, 4-day pass $10. Tues.–Sun. 10–5. www.miaclab.org*

★ **⑯ MUSEUM OF INTERNATIONAL FOLK ART.** Everywhere you look in this facility, the premier institution of its kind in the world, you'll find amazingly inventive handmade objects—a tin Madonna, a devil made from bread dough, and all kinds of rag dolls. Florence Dibell Bartlett, who founded the museum in 1953, donated its first 4,000 works. In the late 1970s, Alexander and Susan Girard, major folk-art collectors, gave the museum 106,000 items. The Hispanic Heritage Wing contains art dating from the Spanish colonial period (in New Mexico, 1598–1821) to the present. The 5,000-piece exhibit includes religious works—particularly *bultos* (carved wooden statues of saints) and *retablos* (holy images painted on wood or tin). The objects in the Neutrogena Wing are exhibited by theme rather than by date or country of origin—you might, for instance, find a sheer Eskimo parka alongside a Chinese undergarment made of bamboo and cotton webbing. Lloyd's Treasure Chest, the wing's innovative basement section, provides a behind-the-scenes look at more of this collection. You can rummage about storage drawers, peer into microscopes, and, on occasion, speak with conservators and other museum personnel.

706 Camino Lejo, tel. 505/476–1200. $5, 4-day pass $10 (good at all 4 state museums in Santa Fe). Tues.–Sun. 10–5. www.moifa.org

⑱ SANTA FE CHILDREN'S MUSEUM. Stimulating hands-on exhibits, a solar greenhouse, oversize geometric forms, and a simulated 18-ft mountain-climbing wall all contribute to the museum's popularity with kids. Puppeteers and storytellers occasionally perform. 1050 Old Pecos Trail, tel. 505/989–8359. $3. Sept.–May, Thurs.–Sat. 10–5, Sun. noon–5; June–Aug., Wed.–Sat. 10–5, Sun. noon–5.

⑰ WHEELWRIGHT MUSEUM OF THE AMERICAN INDIAN. A private institution in a building shaped like a traditional octagonal Navajo hogan, the Wheelwright opened in 1937. Founded by Boston scholar Mary Cabot Wheelwright and Navajo medicine man Hasteen Klah, the museum originated as a place to house ceremonial materials. Those items are not on view to the public. On display are 19th- and 20th-century baskets, pottery, sculpture, weavings, and paintings, including contemporary works by Native American artists. The Case Trading Post on the lower level is modeled after the trading posts that dotted the Southwestern frontier more than 100 years ago. It carries an extensive selection of books and contemporary Native American jewelry, weaving, and pottery. 704 Camino Lejo, tel. 505/982–4636. Free. Mon.–Sat. 10–5, Sun. 1–5.

HISTORIC GUADALUPE RAILROAD DISTRICT

The historic warehouse district of Santa Fe is commonly referred to as the Railyard District. After the demise of the train route through town, the low-lying warehouses were converted to artist studios and antiques shops. Bookstores, shops, and restaurants have sprung up in the last 15 years. The restored scenic train line is once again putting the town's old depot to use. The local farmers' market turns the depot parking lot into a colorful outdoor fiesta of chiles, fresh greens, lavender, medicinal oils, baked goods, coffee, ranchero music, and socializing, beginning the first weekend in May and continuing through the first weekend in November. It takes place Saturday mornings until noon and Tuesdays as well, from July through September.

Sights to See

⑳ SANTA FE SOUTHERN RAILWAY. For a leisurely tour across the Santa Fe plateau and into the vast Galisteo Basin, where panoramic views extend for up to 120 mi, take a nostalgic ride on the antique cars of the Santa Fe Southern Railway. The train once served a spur of the Atchison, Topeka, & Santa Fe Railway. In 1991, the train started taking visitors on 36-mi round-trip scenic trips to Lamy, a sleepy town without streetlights, offering picnics under the cottonwoods (bring your own or buy one from the caterer that meets the train) at the quaint Lamy train station. Aside from day trips, the railway offers special events such as a Friday-night "High Desert High Ball" cash bar with appetizers, and a "Sunset Run" on which a barbecue, a campfire, and live entertainment await you at the Lamy depot. Trains depart from the Santa Fe Depot, rebuilt in 1909 after the original was destroyed in a fire. *410 S. Guadalupe St., tel. 800/989–8600. Day trips start at $25, Sunset Run starts at $45. Departs May–Oct., Tues.–Thurs. and Sat. 10:30 AM, returns 2:30–3:30; Sun.–Mon. departs 1, returns 4:30 (bring your own refreshments). Sunset Run departs between 6 and 7:15. Call for winter schedule, Sunset Run, and High Desert High Ball times.*

⑲ SANTUARIO DE GUADALUPE. A humble adobe structure built by Franciscan missionaries between 1776 and 1795, this is the oldest shrine in the United States to Our Lady of Guadalupe, patron saint of Mexico. The sanctuary, now a nonprofit cultural center, has adobe walls nearly 3 ft thick. Among the sanctuary's religious art and artifacts is a priceless 16th-century work by Venetian painter Leonardo de Ponte Bassano that depicts Jesus driving the money changers from the temple. Also of note is a portrait of Our Lady of

Guadalupe by the Mexican colonial painter José de Alzíbar. Other highlights are the traditional New Mexican carved and painted altar screen, an authentic 19th-century sacristy, a pictorial-history archive, a library devoted to Archbishop Jean Baptiste Lamy that is furnished with many of his belongings, and a garden with plants from the Holy Land. *100 Guadalupe St., tel. 505/988–2027. Donation suggested. May–Oct., Mon.–Sat. 9–4; Nov.–Apr., weekdays 9–4.*

㉑ **SITE SANTA FE.** The events at this nexus of international contemporary art include lectures, concerts, author readings, performance art, and gallery shows. The facility hosts a biennial exhibition every odd-numbered year. *1606 Paseo de Peralta, tel. 505/989–1199. $5, free Fri. Wed.–Thurs. and weekends 10–5, Fri. 10–7.*

EATING OUT

Santa Fe cuisine is a robust mixture of Pueblo, Spanish, Mexican, and Continental influences. Chefs at European-style cafés prepare superb Mexican dishes; nouvelle New Mexican cuisine is served at elegant restaurants. Hamburgers and comfort food abound at many of the contemporary grills, which manage to bring a unique Santa Fe spin to tried-and-true American cooking. For price categories, *see* the chart *under* Dining *in* Practical Information.

AMERICAN

$$$–$$$$ EL NIDO. Since the 1920s, Santa Feans have made the 6-mi drive to the village of Tesuque to eat at this former dance hall and trading post, which has a cozy ambience and a solid menu of choice aged beef, fresh seafood, and local specialties like chunky green-chile stew. Only a five-minute drive from the Santa Fe Opera, El Nido is a favorite of opera fans. Reservations are recommended during July and August. *U.S. 285/84, 6 mi north of Santa Fe to first Tesuque exit, then about ¼ mi farther to restaurant, tel. 505/988–4340. AE, DC, MC, V. Closed Mon. No lunch.*

$$$–$$$$ **VANESSIE.** An à la carte menu specializing in high-quality cuts of
★ meat, fresh fish, and very simple side dishes is ideally suited for
conservative tastes. The oak interior, high ceilings, and oversize
windows give the restaurant a lodgelike atmosphere. Casual fare
such as large burgers and onion loaf is served in the adjoining
piano bar. Professional pianists perform classical to Broadway
favorites nightly starting at 8 (no cover charge). *434 W. San Francisco
St., tel. 505/982–9966. AE, DC, MC, V.*

AMERICAN/CASUAL

$$–$$$ **ZIA DINER.** This slick diner with a low-key, art deco–style interior
provides a menu that pleases meat-loaf lovers and vegetarians,
senior citizens and families. Stop in for a full meal (try one of their
weeknight blue-plate specials, like Friday night's Pescado Vera
Cruz) or just a thick slice of fresh strawberry-rhubarb pie. Service
is fast and friendly, and the food is fresh and more imaginative
than most diner fare. Patio dining is also available. Reservations
are accepted for parties of six or more. *326 S. Guadalupe St., Railyard
District, tel. 505/988–7008. AE, MC, V.*

$$ **PLAZA CAFÉ.** Run with homespun care by the Razatos family
★ since 1947, this café has been a fixture on the Plaza since 1918.
The decor—red leather banquettes, black Formica tables, tile
floors, vintage Santa Fe photos, a coffered tin ceiling, and a 1940s-
style service counter—hasn't changed much in the past half
century. Standard American fare is served, along with New Mexican
and Greek dishes. A bowl of green chile and beans will leave your
tongue burning—that's the way the locals like it. You can cool it
off with an old-fashioned ice-cream treat from the soda fountain.
All in all, it's a good stop for breakfast, lunch, or dinner. *54 Lincoln
Ave., tel. 505/982–1664. Reservations not accepted. AE, D, MC, V.*

$–$$ **BERT'S BURGER BOWL.** This tiny place has been serving up
yummy charbroiled burgers since the 1950s. The No. 6 (green chile
with cheese) is a staple. You can also get excellent pressure-
cooked chicken, *carne adovada* (red chile–marinated pork), crispy

santa fe dining

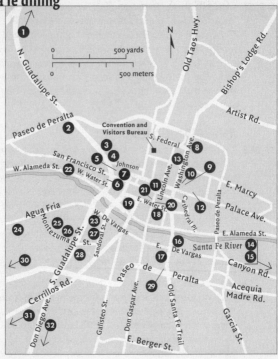

fries, and old-fashioned shakes. There are tables outside and a few chairs indoors. *235 N. Guadalupe St., tel. 505/982–0215. No credit cards.*

$–$$ DAVE'S NOT HERE. Dave may not be here, but you will find one of Santa Fe's best burgers, served with heaps of onions, mushrooms, avocado, or cheese. The cooks at Dave's prepare super made-from-scratch chiles rellenos. For dessert try the slab of deep chocolate cake. *1115 Hickox St. (the extension of Paseo de Peralta west from St. Francis Dr.), tel. 505/983–7060. Reservations not accepted. No credit cards. Closed Sun.*

$ SAVEUR. Fresh ingredients, pleasant atmosphere, and great bread make this a good place for an inexpensive meal just a short walk from the Plaza. In the morning, make your own omelet; in the afternoon, build your own sandwich. Try a daily special, like Friday's grilled tuna with roasted red peppers. *204 Montezuma, where Montezuma intersects with Galisteo/Sandoval, tel. 505/989–4200. Reservations not accepted. D, MC, V. Closed weekends.*

CONTEMPORARY

$$$$ BISTRO 315. As if it were on a thoroughfare in Paris rather than on the Old Santa Fe Trail, Bistro 315 has a Continental, white-tablecloth sophistication, but the offbeat wall art gives it a contemporary feel. Chef and owner Louis Maskow prepares bistro fare using organic vegetables, locally raised beef and lamb, free-range chicken, and fresh seafood. Seasonal specialties on the ever-evolving menu might include duckling with porcini mushroom turnover. The patio opens onto the street scene. *315 Old Santa Fe Trail, tel. 505/986–9190. Reservations essential. AE, MC, V. No lunch Sun.*

$$$$ COYOTE CAFE. The Coyote gives Southwest style a dose of Hollywood with a bold decor that creates its own special effects. The inventive menu is the creation of chef-owner Mark Miller. Try "The Cowboy," a 22-ounce rib eye steak served with barbecued black beans and onion rings dusted with red chile; the short stack of griddled corn cakes with *chipotle* (a hot, smoky chile) shrimp appetizer; or the ravioli filled with sausage made of wild boar and goat cheese. The open dining room can be loud, and it's the kind of place where people go to be seen. On the wine list are more than 500 vintages. Exotic but much less expensive dishes are served on the Rooftop Cantina April through October. The Coyote General Store, under the café, sells Southwestern foodstuffs and Miller's cookbooks. *132 W. Water St., tel. 505/983–1615. AE, D, DC, MC, V. Closed Tues.–Wed. Jan.–Feb.*

$$$$ GERONIMO. Chef Eric DiStefano changes the menu frequently at
★ this restaurant in the Borrego House, which dates from 1756. A typical meal might start with an appetizer like cold water lobster tail on angel hair pasta. Entrées are artful, like mesquite-grilled elk tenderloin with smoked bacon and chestnut strudel, or red-corn relleno with duck and black-bean sauce. The Sunday brunch is also impressive. The intimate, white dining rooms have beamed ceilings, wood floors, fireplaces, and cushioned *bancos* (benches built into the plastered walls). In summer you can dine under the front portal; in winter the bar and fireplace are inviting. *724 Canyon Rd., tel. 505/982–1500. AE, MC, V. No lunch Mon.*

$$$$ OLD HOUSE. Chef Martin Rios changes the menu every Thursday
★ at his fashionably casual restaurant inside the equally fashionable Eldorado Hotel (☞ Where to Stay, *below*). Entrées have included barbecued breast of quail on a crispy corn cake and rack of lamb in a pepita-garlic crust. More than two dozen of the impressive wines are served by the glass. A separate dining room has a slightly more refined interior than the hacienda ambience of the main dining room. Reservations are essential during summer and on weekends year-round. *Eldorado Hotel, 309 W. San Francisco St., tel. 505/988–4455. AE, D, DC, MC, V. Closed Mon. No lunch.*

$$$$ SANTACAFÉ. Minimal elegance marks the interior of Santacafé,
★ one of Santa Fe's vanguard "food as art" restaurants, two blocks north of the Plaza in the historic Padre Gallegos House. Seasonal ingredients, like locally harvested fresh porcini mushrooms, are

included in the inventive dishes. The shrimp and spinach dumplings and shiitake mushroom and cactus spring rolls are particularly good. The patio is a joy in summer. *231 Washington Ave., tel. 505/984–1788. AE, MC, V.*

$$$–$$$$ **ORE HOUSE ON THE PLAZA.** Popular more for its perfect location overlooking the Plaza than for its cuisine, this restaurant serves salmon, swordfish, lobster, ceviche, and steaks that are adequate if uninspired. The specialty margaritas, though, are anything but ordinary: they come in more than 80 flavors, from cool watermelon to zippy jalapeño. *50 Lincoln Ave., upstairs on the southwest corner of the Plaza, tel. 505/983–8687. AE, MC, V.*

$$$–$$$$ **RISTRA.** Continental dishes receive Southwestern accents here— mussels in chipotle-and-mint broth, rack of lamb with creamed garlic potatoes, and perfectly grilled salmon. The wines are well selected and the service is swift and courteous. Navajo blankets hang on stark white walls, and Pueblo pottery adorns the handful of niches. *548 Agua Fria St., near the Railyard District, tel. 505/982– 8608. AE, MC, V. No lunch.*

ECLECTIC

$$$–$$$$ **PINK ADOBE.** Rosalea Murphey opened her restaurant back in
★ 1944, and the place still seems to reflect a time when fewer than 20,000 people lived in town. The intimate, rambling rooms have fireplaces and artwork and are filled with conversation made over special-occasion meals. The ambience of the restaurant, rather than the food, accounts for much of its popularity. The steak Dunnigan, smothered in green chile and mushrooms, and the savory shrimp Louisianne—fat and deep-fried crispy—are among the Continental, New Orleans Creole, and New Mexican dishes served. The apple pie drenched in rum sauce is a favorite. Particularly strong margaritas are mixed in the adjacent Dragon Room bar. Reservations are essential for dinner during the

summer. *406 Old Santa Fe Trail, tel. 505/983–7712. AE, D, DC, MC, V. No lunch weekends.*

FRENCH

$$$–$$$$ **ROCIADA.** Country French has arrived in Santa Fe with this intimate bistro, which opened in 2000. Fresh ingredients are used for the Provençal specialties, including a delicious onion soup *velouté*, which combines five types of onions in a light cream and vegetable broth base. Another specialty is the chilled bisque of crawfish and corn. The list of French wines is extensive. *304 Johnson St., tel. 505/983–3800. AE, D, MC, V. Closed Mon. No lunch.*

INDIAN

$$ **INDIA PALACE.** East Indian cuisine was utterly foreign to most locals before the arrival of India Palace, but many Santa Feans have since become devotees of chef Bal Dev Singh's spicy dishes. The serene deep-pink interior sets the scene for tender tandoori chicken and lamb and superb curried seafood and vegetables. Meals are cooked as hot or mild as you wish, and vegetarian dishes are prepared. For lunch, try the Indian buffet to sample some of their staple dishes. *227 Don Gaspar Ave., at the rear of the El Centro shopping center, tel. 505/986–5859. AE, D, MC, V.*

ITALIAN

$$–$$$ **ANDIAMO.** Produce from the Farmers' Market across the street adds to the seasonal surprises of this intimate restaurant inspired by northern Italian cuisine. Fresh ingredients, natural meats, and homemade desserts are guaranteed. Try the crispy polenta with rosemary and Gorgonzola sauce for an appetizer and, if you want to go casual, a pizza or, for heartier fare, the linguine *puttanesca* with grilled tuna. *322 Garfield St., near the Railyard District, tel. 505/995–9595. AE, DC, MC, V. Closed Tues. Oct.–May. No lunch.*

$$–$$$ **IL PIATTO.** Creative pasta dishes like risotto with duck, artichoke, and truffle oil and homemade pumpkin ravioli grace the menu here. Entrées include pancetta-wrapped trout and roast chicken with Italian sausage. *95 W. Marcy St., tel. 505/984–1091. AE, MC, V. No lunch weekends.*

$$ PRANZO ITALIAN GRILL. Northern Italy with a touch of cream is the signature of the pastas on the menu. Try the *frito misto* (fried scallops, shrimp, and calamari with marinara sauce—plenty for two to three people). There's a large variety of individually sized, thin-crust pizzas, as well as mixed green salads. Upstairs, full meals are served on the rooftop terrace overlooking the Railyard area. You can hear the church bells ringing if you happen to be dining around 6 PM. *540 Montezuma Ave., Railyard District, tel. 505/984–2645. AE, DC, MC, V. No lunch Sun.*

JAPANESE

$$–$$$ SHOHKO. Tasty tempura—including a Southwestern variation made with green chile—and more than 35 kinds of sushi are served at this small Japanese restaurant. At the 16-seat sushi bar you can watch the masters at work. *321 Johnson St., tel. 505/983–7288. AE, D, MC, V. No lunch weekends.*

LATIN

$$$$ CAFE PASQUAL'S. A block southwest of the Plaza, this cheerful
★ cubbyhole dishes up regional and Latin American specialties for breakfast, lunch, and dinner. Don't be discouraged by lines out in front—it's worth the wait. The culinary muse behind it all is Katharine Kagel, who for more than 20 years has been introducing specialties like Huevos Motuleños (a concoction of black beans and eggs over a blue corn tortilla, topped with tomatillo sauce and goat cheese) to diners. Dinner is a more formal affair, with Latin meals joined by Asian and French entrées. The Plato Supremo includes a taco of citrus-garlic shrimp, chicken mole puebla, rice, and exotic salad. Mexican folk art and colorful tiles and murals by Oaxacan artist Leo Vigildo Martinez create a festive atmosphere. Try the communal table if you want to be seated in a hurry.

Reservations are accepted for dinner. *121 Don Gaspar Ave., tel. 505/ 983–9340 or 800/722–7672. AE, MC, V.*

$$–$$$ LOS MAYAS. Owners Fernando Antillas and Reyes Solano brought the spirit of Latin America with them when they opened this restaurant in 1998. They've transformed a nondescript building into a cozy setting with a patio. The menu offers a taste of the Americas. Try the enchilada banana, a baked plantain served with mole. There is music every night, including a harp player from Paraguay and a rollicking accordion player from Santa Fe. Ask Fernando to sing—he has a voice that harks back to old Mexico. *409 W. Water St., at northwest corner of intersection with Guadalupe St., tel. 505/986–9930. AE, D, MC, V. No lunch Oct.–Apr.*

MEDITERRANEAN

$$–$$$ WHISTLING MOON CAFE. Unusual spices scent the Mediterranean fare, which includes pasta calamari, Greek salad, a Middle Eastern sampler, and grilled duck. The coriander-cumin fries are irresistible, as is the homemade Greek honey cheesecake. Although the small ocher dining room with red Moroccan weavings is a touch noisy, the food and prices more than make up for it. On weekends a brunch of traditional standards like eggs Benedict and omelets is served. There's also patio dining. *402 N. Guadalupe St., tel. 505/ 983–3093. Reservations essential for 6 or more. MC, V.*

MEXICAN

$$–$$$ GUADALUPE CAFÉ. Come to this informal café for hefty servings of New Mexican favorites like enchiladas and quesadillas, topped off with *sopaipillas* (fluffy fried bread). The seasonal raspberry pancakes are one of many breakfast favorites. *422 Old Santa Fe Trail, tel. 505/982–9762. Reservations not accepted. AE, D, DC, MC, V.*

$$–$$$ MARIA'S NEW MEXICAN KITCHEN. Maria's is proud to serve a walloping 80 kinds of tequila, and Jose Cuervo is the low end of the high-quality offerings. All but six of the tequilas are 100% agave.

Diners enjoy their margaritas with basic dishes like rellenos, enchiladas, and *carne adovada* (red chile–marinated pork), and, on occasion, to the serenades of strolling guitarists. *555 W. Cordova Rd., tel. 505/983–7929. AE, D, DC, MC, V.*

$$–$$$ OLD MEXICO GRILL. For a taste of Old Mexico in New Mexico,
★ sample dishes like *arracheras* (the traditional name for fajitas) and tacos *al carbón* (shredded pork cooked in a mole sauce and folded into corn tortillas). Start the meal with a fresh ceviche appetizer and a cool lime margarita. The location in a shopping center makes parking a snap. *2434 Cerrillos Rd., College Plaza S, tel. 505/473–0338. Reservations not accepted. D, MC, V. No lunch weekends.*

SOUTHWESTERN

$$$$ ANASAZI. Soft light illuminates the stone and adobe interior of this restaurant, which became a Santa Fe fixture the day it opened. Chef Randall Warder combines New Mexican and Native American flavors to produce exotic fare like flat bread with fire-roasted sweet peppers, and cinnamon-chile filet mignon chop. The large dining room has wooden tables and bancos upholstered with handwoven textiles from Chimayó. Groups of up to 12 can dine in the private wine cellar, and groups of up to 40 can be served in the romantic library. If you don't want to invest in dinner, try a delicious breakfast. The Sunday brunch is excellent. *113 Washington Ave., tel. 505/988–3236. AE, D, DC, MC, V.*

$$$$ LA CASA SENA. The Southwestern and Continental fare served at La Casa Sena is rich and beautifully presented. Weather permitting, get a table on the patio surrounded by hollyhocks, flowering shrubs, and centuries-old adobe walls. If you order the *trucha en terra-cotta* (fresh trout wrapped in corn husks and baked in clay), ask your waiter to save the clay head for you as a souvenir. Finish dinner with the wonderful citrus mascarpone tart with orange sauce and Grand Marnier–soaked berries. Weekend brunch dishes are equally elegant. For a musical meal (evenings only), sit in the restaurant's adjacent Cantina, where the talented staff belt out Broadway show tunes. Meals in the Cantina are less expensive, and less exciting. Reservations are essential in summer. *Sena Plaza, 125 E. Palace Ave., tel. 505/988–9232. AE, D, DC, MC, V.*

$–$$$ COWGIRL. Part restaurant, part bar, part museum, and part theater, this Western grill serves Texas-style barbecue, good New Mexican fare, hybrid Southwestern dishes such as grilled-salmon soft tacos, and butternut-squash casserole. In summer you can dine on tree-shaded patios and kids can eat in the Corral, a special area with its own menu. After dinner there's entertainment—blues and rock bands, singer-songwriters, or comedians. Brunch is served on weekends. *319 S. Guadalupe St., tel. 505/982–2565. AE, D, MC, V.*

$$–$$$ THE SHED. The lines at lunch attest to the status of this downtown New Mexican eatery. The rambling adobe dating from 1692 is decorated with folk art, and service is downright neighborly. Even if you're a devoted green chile fan, try the locally grown red chile the place is famous for. Specialties include red-chile enchiladas, green-chile stew with potatoes and pork, *posole* (soup made with lime hominy, pork, chile, and garlic), and charbroiled Shedburgers. The homemade desserts are fabulous. Now there's a full bar, too. Reservations are accepted only for parties of six or more. *113½ E. Palace Ave., tel. 505/982–9030. AE, DC, MC, V. Closed Sun. No dinner Mon.–Wed.*

SPANISH

$$–$$$ EL FAROL. In this crossover cuisine town, owner David Salazar sums up his food in one word: "Spanish." Order a classic entrée like paella or make a meal from the 20 different tapas—from tiny fried squid to wild mushrooms. Dining is indoors and outdoors. Touted as the oldest restaurant and cantina in Santa Fe, El Farol (built in 1835) has a relaxed ambience, a unique blend of the Western frontier and contemporary Santa Fe. People push back the chairs and start dancing at around 9:30. The bar is smoky and noisy but unnoticeable from the back dining room thanks to the ventilating system and thick adobe walls. *808 Canyon Rd., tel. 505/983–9912. D, DC, MC, V.*

SHOPPING

Santa Fe has been a trading post for a long time. A thousand years ago the great pueblos of the Anasazi civilizations were strategically located between the buffalo-hunting tribes of the Great Plains and the Indians of Mexico. Native Americans in New Mexico traded turquoise, which was thought to have magical properties, and other valuables with Indians from Mexico for metals, shells, parrots, and other exotic items. After the arrival of the Spanish and the subsequent development of the West, Santa Fe became the place to exchange silver from Mexico and natural resources from New Mexico—including hides, fur, and foodstuffs—for manufactured goods, whiskey, and greenbacks from the United States. With the building of the railroad in 1880, Santa Fe had access to all kinds of manufactured goods as well as those unique to the region via the old trade routes.

The trading legacy remains, but now downtown Santa Fe caters almost exclusively to those looking for handcrafted goods. Sure, T-shirt outlets and major retail clothing shops have moved in, but shopping in Santa Fe remains a unique experience for most visitors. The enigma of Santa Fe style, as distinct as the city's architecture, continues, although in a tempered, more so-phisticated version than a decade ago, when chile ristras and wooden howling coyotes took over the shops.

Santa Fe is a great place to window shop, perhaps because of the high visual standards such an artistic community commands. It is a town where color, texture, and pattern make a brave stand for diversity rather than uniformity. Canyon Road, where art galleries are within a short distance of one another, is the perfect place to find one-of-a-kind gifts and collectibles. The downtown

santa fe shopping

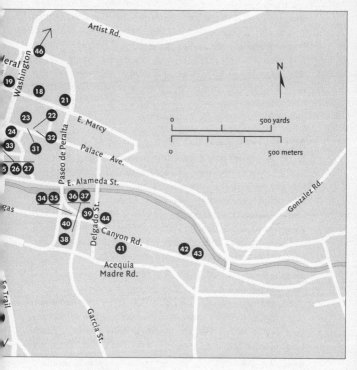

Morning Star
Gallery, **44**

Nedra Matteucci
Galleries, **38**

Nicholas
Potter, **32**

Niman Fine
Arts, **17**

Origins, **15**

Ornament of
Santa Fe, **9**

Pachamama, **35**

Packard's on the
Plaza, **24**

Photo-Eye
Books, **36**

Photo-Eye
Gallery, **37**

Plan B Evolving
Arts, **45**

The Rainbow
Man, **31**

Relics of the Old
West, **29**

Riva Yares
Gallery, **16**

Santa Fe Boot
Company, **1**

Shidoni Foundry
and Galleries, **46**

Simply
Santa Fe, **27**

Trade Roots
Collection, **20**

Western
Warehouse, **2, 5**

William R. Talbot
Fine Art, **14**

Wyeth Hurd
Gallery, **21**

district, around the Plaza, has unusual gift shops, clothing and shoe stores that range from theatrical to conventional, curio shops, and art galleries. The Historic Guadalupe Railroad District, popularly referred to as the Railyard District, includes Sanbusco Market Place on the southwest perimeter of downtown. It's a laid-back place to mingle with residents who don't want to fight for a parking place near the Plaza. All areas have cafés and restaurants that satisfy the need to people-watch and relax.

ART GALLERIES

The following are only a few of the more than 150 galleries in Santa Fe—with the best of representational, nonobjective, Native American, Latin American, cutting edge, photographic, and soulful works that defy categorization. The Santa Fe Convention and Visitors Bureau has a more extensive listing. *The Wingspread Collectors Guide to Santa Fe and Taos* is a good resource and is available in hotels. Check the *Pasatiempo* pullout in the *Santa Fe New Mexican* on Friday for a preview of gallery openings.

Andrew Smith Gallery (203 W. San Francisco St., tel. 505/984–1234) is a significant photo gallery dealing in works by Edward S. Curtis and other 19th-century chroniclers of the American West. Major figures from the 20th and 21st centuries are Ansel Adams, Eliot Porter, Alfred Stieglitz, Annie Liebowitz, and regional artists like Barbara Van Cleve.

Bellas Artes (653 Canyon Rd., tel. 505/983–2745), a sophisticated gallery and sculpture garden, has ancient ceramics and represents internationally renowned artists like Judy Pfaff, Phoebe Adams, and Olga de Amaral.

Charlotte Jackson Fine Art (123 E. Marcy St., tel. 505/989–8688) focuses primarily on monochromatic "radical" painting. Florence Pierce, Joe Barnes, Anne Cooper, and Joseph Marionni are among the artists producing minimalist works dealing with light and space.

Dewey Galleries (Catron Building, 53 Old Santa Fe Trail, tel. 505/982–8632) shows historic Navajo textiles and jewelry, pueblo pottery, and antique Spanish colonial furniture, as well as paintings and sculpture.

Ernesto Mayans Gallery (601 Canyon Rd., tel. 983-8068) focuses on paintings and works on paper. There's an excellent selection of contemporary photography by Mexican luminaries Graciela Iturbide and Manuel Alvarez Bravo.

Gerald Peters Gallery (1011 Paseo de Peralta, tel. 505/954–5700) is Santa Fe's leading gallery of American and European art from the 19th century to the present. It has works by Charles M. Russell, Albert Bierstadt, the Taos Society, the New Mexico Modernists, and Georgia O'Keeffe, as well as contemporary artists.

Guadalupe Fine Art (403 Canyon Rd., across the courtyard in back, tel. 505/982–2403) is a vibrant venue for emerging and established painters and sculptors. Owner and gallery artist Lena Bartula hosts annual, thematic group shows that are community events. The Southwest Zen-style sculpture garden is a great place to linger.

James Kelly Contemporary Gallery (1601 Paseo de Peralta, tel. 505/989–1601) displays works by such internationally renowned artists as Susan Rothenberg and video artist Bruce Nauman in its warehouse space.

LewAllen Contemporary (129 W. Palace Ave., tel. 505/988–8997) is a leading center for a variety of contemporary arts by Southwest artists. Arlene LewAllen has been a vital force in the Santa Fe art scene for more than 20 years.

Meredith-Kelly Gallery (135 W. Palace Ave., tel. 505/986–8699) shows work by Latin American artists, some local, working mostly in painting. Most of the work is global in theme rather than culturally specific. Zuñega is one of the big names.

Nedra Matteucci Galleries (1075 Paseo de Peralta, tel. 505/ 982–4631) exhibits works by California regionalists, members of the early Taos and Santa Fe schools, and masters of American Impressionism and Modernism. Spanish-colonial furniture, Indian antiquities, and a fantastic sculpture garden are other draws of this well-respected establishment.

Niman Fine Arts (125 Lincoln Ave., tel. 505/988–5091) focuses on the prolific work of two contemporary Native American artists—Hopi painter Dan Namingha and the late Apache sculptor Allan Houser.

Photo-Eye Gallery (370 Garcia St., tel. 505/988–5152) shows everything from contemporary photography that includes the beautiful and sublime to controversial works by Jock Sturges.

Plan B Evolving Arts (1050 Old Pecos Trail, tel. 505/982–1338) showcases young artists, with an emphasis on cutting-edge and avant-garde works.

Riva Yares Gallery (123 Grant St, tel. 505/984–0330) specializes in contemporary artists of Latin American descent. There are sculptures by California artist Manuel Neri, color field paintings by Esteban Vicente, and works by Santa Feans Elias Rivera, Rico Eastman, and others.

Shidoni Foundry and Galleries (Bishop's Lodge Rd., Tesuque, 5 mi north of Santa Fe, tel. 505/988–8001) casts work for accomplished and emerging artists from all over North America. On the grounds of an old chicken ranch, Shidoni has a rambling sculpture garden and a gallery. Guided tours of the foundry take place on Saturday.

William R. Talbot Fine Art (129 W. San Francisco St., tel. 505/ 982–1559) sells antique maps and prints.

Wyeth Hurd Gallery (229 E. Marcy St., tel. 505/989–8380) carries the work of the multigenerational arts family that includes N. C. Wyeth; his children Andrew and Henriette Wyeth;

Peter Hurd, Henriette's husband; Michael Hurd, son of Henriette and Peter; Jamie Wyeth, Andrew's son; and Peter de la Fuente, Henriette and Peter's grandson. Works include the landscape of the Delaware River valley that so inspired the Wyeth family and the New Mexico landscapes of Peter Hurd, who grew up in Roswell.

FLEA MARKETS

Tesuque Pueblo Flea Market (U.S. 84/285, 7 mi north of Santa Fe), formerly known as Trader Jack's or the Santa Fe Flea Market, was once considered the best flea market in America by its loyal legion of bargain hunters. The Tesuque Pueblo now manages the market and has made a few changes. Occult services, such as palm reading, are gone, and higher vendor fees have cut down on garage-sale treasures and increased the predictable goods brought in by professional flea-market dealers. You can still find everything from a half-wolf puppy or African carvings to vintage cowboy boots, fossils, or a wall clock made out of an old hubcap. On 12 acres of land belonging to the Tesuque Pueblo, the market is right next to the Santa Fe Opera and is open Friday through Sunday, May through October, and weekends in November, December, and mid-February through April.

SPECIALTY STORES
Books

More than 20 stores in Santa Fe sell used books, and a handful of high-quality shops carry the latest releases from mainstream and small presses.

Allá (102 W. San Francisco St., upstairs, tel. 505/988–5416) is one of Santa Fe's most delightful small bookstores. It focuses on hard-to-find Spanish-language books and records, including limited-edition handmade books from Central America. It also carries Native American books and music, as well as English translations.

Collected Works Book Store (208B W. San Francisco St., tel. 505/988–4226) carries art and travel books, including a generous selection of books on Southwestern art, architecture, and general history, as well as the latest in contemporary literature.

Nicholas Potter (211 E. Palace Ave., tel. 505/983–5434) specializes in used, rare, and out-of-print books. The quixotic shop also stocks used jazz and classical CDs.

Photo-Eye Books (376 Garcia St., tel. 505/988–5152) stocks new, rare, and out-of-print photography books.

Clothing

Women have been known to arrive here in Liz Claiborne and leave in a broomstick skirt and Navajo velvet shirt. Men, who swore they never would, don silver *bolo* ties. Function dictates form in cowboy fashions. A wide-brimmed hat is essential in open country for protection from heat, rain, and insects. In the Southwest there's no such thing as a stingy brim. Cowboy hats made by Resistol, Stetson, Bailey, and other leading firms cost between $50 and $500, and hats made of fur and other exotic materials can fetch four figures. Small wonder that when it rains in Santa Fe or Albuquerque, some people are more concerned about protecting their hats than about getting wet.

The pointed toes of cowboy boots slide easily in and out of stirrups, and high heels help keep feet in the stirrups. Tall tops protect ankles and legs on rides through brush and cactus country and can protect the wearer from a nasty shin bruise from a skittish horse.

Some Western fashion accessories were once purely functional. A colorful bandanna protected an Old West cowboy from sun- and windburn and served as a mask in windstorms, when riding drag behind a herd or, on occasions far rarer than Hollywood would have us believe, when robbing trains. A cowboy's sleeveless vest enhanced his ability to maneuver during roping and riding chores and provided pocket space that his skintight pants—snug to prevent wrinkles in the saddle area—didn't. Belt buckles are probably the most sought-after accessories— gold ones go for as much as $1,000.

Back at the Ranch (235 Don Gaspar, tel. 505/989–8110 or 888/ 962–6687) is a musty old shop stocked with used cowboy boots, from red leather to turquoise snakeskin. Some things get better with age, especially cowboy boots.

Jane Smith (550 Canyon Rd., tel. 505/988–4775) sells extraordinary handmade Western wear for women and men, from cowboy boots and sweaters to Plains Indians–style beaded tunics.

Mirá (101 W. Marcy St., tel. 505/988–3585) clothing for women is slick, eclectic, and funky, combining the adventurous spirit of Mexico with global contemporary fashion. The shop has accessories and collectibles from Latin America, hemp apparel, and knockout vintage-inspired dresses.

Montecristi Custom Hat Works (322 McKenzie St., tel. 505/ 983–9598) is where the smart set goes for custom-made straw hats so snug they're all but guaranteed to stay on, even in an open convertible.

Origins (135 W. San Francisco St., tel. 505/988–2323) borrows from many cultures, carrying pricey women's wear like antique kimonos and custom-dyed silk jackets. One-of-a-kind accessories complete the spectacular look that Santa Fe inspires.

Santa Fe Boot Company (950 W. Cordova Rd., tel. 505/983– 8415) stocks boots by all major manufacturers and more exotic styles designed by owner Marian Trujillo. Hats and Western outerwear are also sold.

Simply Santa Fe (72 E. San Francisco St., tel. 505/988–3100) carries unusual and lovely items, such as cut velvet vests with handmade buttons, turquoise and coral watchbands, and hand-beaded evening bags. It also carries fine furnishings like leather wing chairs and forged steel beds.

Western Warehouse (De Vargas Center, tel. 505/982–3388; Villa Linda Mall, tel. 505/471–8775) sells all the top-name hats, boots, belts, and buckles.

Home Furnishings

Artesanos (222 Galisteo St. and 1414 Maclovia St., tel. 505/471–8020) is one of the best Mexican-import shops in the nation, with everything from leather chairs to papier-mâché *calaveras* (skeletons used in Day of the Dead celebrations), tinware, and Talavera tiles.

Doodlet's (120 Don Gaspar Ave., tel. 505/983–3771) has an eclectic collection of stuff: pop-up books, bizarre postcards, tin art, hooked rugs, and stringed lights. Wonderment is in every display case, drawing the eye to the unusual.

Foreign Traders (202 Galisteo St., tel. 505/983–6441), a Santa Fe institution founded as the Old Mexico Shop in 1927 and still run by the same family, stocks handicrafts, antiques, and accessories from Mexico and other parts of the world.

Jackalope (2820 Cerrillos Rd., tel. 505/471–8539) sprawls over 7 acres, incorporating several pottery barns, a furniture store, endless aisles of knickknacks from Latin America and Asia, and a huge greenhouse. There's a lunch counter, barnyard animals, and a prairie-dog village.

Montez Gallery (Sena Plaza Courtyard, 125 E. Palace Ave., tel. 505/982–1828) sells Hispanic works of religious art and decoration, including *retablos, bultos,* furniture, paintings, pottery, weavings, and jewelry.

Pachamama (223 Canyon Rd., tel. 505/983–4020) carries Latin American folk art, including small tin or silver *milagros,* the stamped metal images used as votive offerings. Milagro-inspired jewelry by Elena Solow, which combines gemstones with antique-looking images in stamped silver, is a rare find. The shop also carries weavings and Spanish-colonial antiques, including santos, devotional carvings, and painted images of saints.

Jewelry

Karen Melfi Collection (225 Canyon Rd, tel. 505/982–3032) sells high-quality yet moderately priced handmade jewelry and other wearable art.

Ornament of Santa Fe (209 W. San Francisco, tel. 505/983–9399) is full of cosmopolitan jewelry and unique hair accessories. Precious and semiprecious stones set in gold and silver push the envelope of tradition without being trendy.

Native American Arts and Crafts

Cristof's (420 Old Santa Fe Trail, tel. 505/988–9881) has a large selection of pottery, sculpture, and contemporary Navajo weavings and sand paintings.

Joshua Baer & Co. (116½ E. Palace Ave., tel. 505/988–8944) carries superb historic Navajo textiles and rare antique Pueblo weavings.

Morning Star Gallery (513 Canyon Rd., tel. 505/982–8187) is a veritable museum of Native American art and artifacts. An adobe shaded by a huge cottonwood tree houses antique basketry, pre-1940 Navajo silver jewelry, Northwest Coast Native American carvings, Navajo weavings, and art of the Plains Indians.

Packard's on the Plaza (61 Old Santa Fe Trail, tel. 505/983–9241), the oldest Native American arts-and-crafts store on Santa Fe Plaza, sells Zapotec Indian rugs from Mexico and original rug designs by Richard Enzer, old pottery, saddles, kachina dolls, and an excellent selection of coral and turquoise jewelry.

The **Rainbow Man** (107 E. Palace Ave., tel. 505/982–8706), established in 1945, does business in the remains of a building that was damaged during the 1680 Pueblo Revolt. The shop carries early Navajo, Mexican, and Chimayó textiles, along with photographs by Edward S. Curtis, vintage pawn jewelry, and katsinas.

Relics of the Old West (402 Old Santa Fe Trail, tel. 505/989–7663) stocks eclectic crafts and artifacts from cowboy-and-Indian days, as well as high-end Navajo textiles, old and new. Navajo weavers are on-site demonstrating their craft during the summer.

Trade Roots Collection (411 Paseo de Peralta, tel. 505/982–8168) sells Native American ritual objects, such as fetish jewelry and Hopi rattles. The store is a good source of craft materials.

OUTDOOR ACTIVITIES AND SPORTS

The Sangre de Cristo Mountains (the name translates as "Blood of Christ" for the red glow they radiate at sunset) preside over northern New Mexico, constant and gentle reminders of the mystery and power of the natural world. To the south, the landscape descends into the high desert of north-central New Mexico. The dramatic shifts in elevation and topography make for a wealth of outdoor activities. Head to the mountains for fishing, camping, and skiing; to the nearby Rio Grande for kayaking and rafting; and almost anywhere in the area for bird-watching and biking.

PARTICIPANT SPORTS
Bicycling

A map of bike trips—among them a 30-mi round-trip ride from downtown Santa Fe to Ski Santa Fe at the end of Highway 475—can be picked up at the **Santa Fe Convention and Visitors Bureau** (201 W. Marcy St., tel. 505/984–6760) or the **New**

Mexico Public Lands Information Center (☞ Campgrounds, *below*).

Bike N' Sport (1829 Cerrillos Rd., tel. 505/820–0809) provides rentals and information about guided tours. **Sun Mountain** (107 Washington Ave., tel. 505/820–2902) provides mountain bikes from its Plaza location. The shop will also deliver to your hotel, any day, year round.

Bird-Watching

At the end of Upper Canyon Road, at the mouth of the canyon as it wends up into the foothills, is the **Randall Davey Audubon Center,** a 135-acre nature sanctuary that harbors diverse birds and other wildlife. An educator leads free nature walks on the first Saturday of each month. The home and studio of Randall Davey, a prolific early Santa Fe artist, is here, and tours of the rambling house are given on summer Monday afternoons. *Top of Upper Canyon Rd., tel. 505/983–4609. $1, house tour $3. Daily 9–5.*

Golf

Marty Sanchez Links de Santa Fe (205 Caja del Rio, off NM 599, tel. 505/438–5200), a relatively new, public 18-hole, par-72 golf course on the high prairie southwest of Santa Fe, has views of mountain ranges. It has driving and putting ranges, a pro shop, and a snack bar. The greens fee is $49 for nonresidents (plus $11 per rider per cart).

The 18-hole, par-72 **Pueblo de Cochiti Golf Course** (5200 Cochiti Hwy., Cochiti Lake, tel. 505/465–2239), set against a backdrop of steep canyons and red-rock mesas, is a 45-minute drive southwest of the city. Cochiti, one of the top public golf courses in the country, has a greens fee of $25 on weekdays and $32 on weekends and holidays; an optional cart costs $11 per person.

Santa Fe Country Club (Airport Rd., tel. 505/471–0601), a tree-shaded semiprivate 18-hole, par-72 golf course, has driving and putting ranges and a pro shop. You can rent clubs and electric carts. The greens fee is $55 for nonresidents, and a cart costs $15 per single rider or $11 for each rider.

Hiking

Hiking around Santa Fe can take you into high-altitude alpine country or into lunaresque high desert as you head south and the elevation drops radically. For winter hiking, the gentler climates to the south are less likely to be snow-packed, while the alpine areas will likely require snowshoes or cross-country skis. In summer, wildflowers are in bloom in the high country and the temperature is generally at least 10 degrees cooler than in town. For information about specific areas, contact the **New Mexico Public Lands Information Center** (☞ Campgrounds, *below*). The **Sierra Club** (621 Old Santa Fe Trail, tel. 505/983–2703) organizes group hikes. You can get information from the pick-up box in front of their office.

The mountain trails accessible at the base of the Ski Santa Fe area (end of Highway 475) offer a refuge from the dry summer heat in town. Weather can change with one gust of wind, so be prepared with extra clothing, rain gear, water, and food. The sun at 10,000 ft is very powerful, even with a hat and sunscreen. **Aspen Vista** is a lovely hike along a south-facing mountainside. Take Hyde Park Road 13 mi, and the trail begins before the ski area. After walking a few miles through thick aspen groves you'll come to panoramic views of Santa Fe. The path is well marked and gently inclines toward Tesuque Peak. The trail becomes shadier with elevation—snow has been reported on the trail as late as July. In winter, after heavy snows, the trail is great for intermediate–advanced cross-country skiing. The round-trip is 12 mi, but it's just 3½ mi to the spectacular overlook. The hillside is covered with golden aspen trees in late September.

Tsankawi Trail, pronounced sank-ah-*wee,* will take you through the ancient rock trails of the Pajarito Plateau. The Pueblo people created the trails in the 1400s as they made their way from their mesa-top homes to the fields and springs in the canyon below. In the 1½-mi loop you'll see petroglyphs and south-facing cave dwellings. Wear good shoes for the rocky path and a climb on a 12-ft ladder that shoots between a crevasse in the rock and the highest point of the mesa. This is an ideal walk if you don't have time to explore Bandelier National Monument (☞ Side Trips from Santa Fe) in depth but want to get a taste of it. It's on the way to Los Alamos, about a 35-minute drive from Santa Fe. *25 mi northwest of Santa Fe. Take US 285/84 north to the Los Alamos exit for NM 502. Go west on 502 until the turnoff for White Rock, Hwy. 4. Continue for several miles to the sign for Tsankawi on the left. The trail is clearly marked. tel. 505/672–3861.*

Tent Rocks is the place to hike if you always wanted to walk on the moon. The sculpted sandstone rock formations look like stacked tents on a stark, water- and wind-eroded hillside. Located 45 minutes south of Santa Fe, near Cochiti Pueblo, Tent Rocks is excellent hiking in dry winter, spring, or fall weather. Avoid it in summer—the rocks magnify the heat. The drive to this magical landscape is equally awesome, as the road heads west toward Cochiti Dam and through the cottonwood groves around the pueblo. It's a good hike for kids. The round-trip hiking distance is only 2 mi, about 1½ hours, but it's the kind of place you'll want to hang out in for a while. Take a camera. *I–25 south to Cochiti exit 264. Go right (west) off the exit ramp on NM 16 for 8 mi. Turn right at the T intersection onto NM 22. Continue approximately 3½ more mi (you will pass Cochiti Pueblo entrance). Turn right on NM 266 "Tent Rocks" and continue 5 mi to the "WELCOME TO TENT ROCKS" sign. The last stretch of road is jarring, washboarded gravel. tel. 505/465–2244. $5 per car.*

Horseback Riding

New Mexico's rugged countryside has been the setting for many Hollywood westerns. Whether you want to ride the range that Gregory Peck and Kevin Costner rode or just head out feeling tall in the saddle, you can do so year-round. Rates average about $20 an hour.

Bishop's Lodge (Bishop's Lodge Rd., tel. 505/983–6377) provides rides and guides from April to November. Call for reservations. Rides with **Broken Saddle Riding Co.** (High Desert Ranch, Cerrillos, tel. 505/470–0074) take you around the old turquoise and silver mines the Cerrillos area is noted for. On a Tennessee Walker or a Missouri Fox Trotter you can explore the Cerrillos hills and canyons, 23 mi southeast of Santa Fe. This is not the usual nose-to-tail trail ride.

Galarosa Stable (Galisteo, tel. 505/983–6565 or 800/338–6877) provides rentals by the half day or full day south of Santa Fe in the panoramic Galisteo Basin. **Vientos Encantados** (Round Barn Stables, off U.S. 84/285, Ojo Caliente, tel. 505/583–2233), a one-hour drive north of Santa Fe, conducts trail rides and pack trips near the Ojo Caliente mineral springs. Reserve at least one day in advance.

River Rafting

If you want to watch birds and wildlife along the banks, try the laid-back Huck Finn floats along the Rio Chama or the Rio Grande's White Rock Canyon. The season is generally between April and September. Most outfitters have overnight package plans, and all offer half- and full-day trips. Be prepared to get wet, and wear secure water shoes. For a list of outfitters who guide trips on the Rio Grande and the Rio Chama, write the **Bureau of Land Management, Taos Resource Area Office** (224 Cruz Alta Rd., Taos 87571, tel. 505/758–8851).

Kokopelli Rafting Adventures (541 Cordova Rd., tel. 505/983–3734 or 800/879–9035) specializes in trips through the relatively mellow White Rock Canyon as well as white water. **New Wave Rafting Company** (103 E. Water St., Suite F, tel. 505/984–1444 or 800/984–1444) conducts full-day, half-day, and overnight river trips, with daily departures from Santa Fe. **Santa Fe Rafting Company and Outfitters** (1000 Cerrillos Rd., tel. 505/988–4914 or 800/467–7238) customizes rafting tours. Tell them what you want—they'll do it.

Running

Because of the city's altitude (7,000 ft), you may feel heavy-legged and light-headed if you start running shortly after you arrive. Once you've become acclimated, though, you'll find that this is a great place to run. There's a jogging path along the Santa Fe River, parallel to Alameda, and another at Fort Marcy on Washington Avenue.

Three races of note take place each year (☞ Santa Fe Convention and Visitors Bureau in Practical Information). The **Santa Fe Runaround,** a 10-km race held in early June, begins and ends at the Plaza. The **Women's Five-Kilometer Run** is held in early August. Runners turn out in droves on Labor Day for the **Old Santa Fe Trail Run.**

Skiing

To save time during the busy holiday season you may want to rent skis or snowboards in town the night before hitting the slopes, or early in the morning so you don't have to waste your pricey lift ticket. **Alpine Sports** (121 Sandoval St., tel. 505/983–5155) rents downhill and cross-country skis and snowboards. **Ski Tech** (905 St. Francis Dr., tel. 505/983–5512) rents the works, including loaner ski racks and snow gear.

Ski Santa Fe (end of Hwy. 475, tel. 505/982–4429), usually open from Thanksgiving to Easter, is a fine, midsize operation that receives an average of 250 inches of snow a year and plenty of sunshine. One of America's highest ski areas—the summit is a little more than 12,000 ft above sea level—it has a variety of terrain and seems bigger than its 1,650 ft of vertical rise and 500 acres. There are some great powder stashes, tough bump runs, and many wide, gentle cruising runs. The 40-plus trails are ranked 20% beginner, 40% intermediate, and 40% advanced. Snowboarders are welcome and there's the Norquist Trail for cross-country skiers. The kids' center, Chipmunk Corner, provides day care for infants and supervised skiing for children. The ski school is excellent. Rentals, a good cafeteria, a ski shop, and Totemoff's bar are other amenities. Call for **snow-condition information** (tel. 505/983–9155, www.skisantafe.com).

Pajarito Mountain Ski Area, a small, low-key area near Los Alamos, has some excellent long runs and a good selection of wide-open, intermediate mogul runs. There's no artificial snowmaking, so the slopes are barely open during dry winters. But there's never a wait in lift lines. Call for **ski information** (tel. 505/662–5725) and **snow-condition information** (tel. 505/662–7669).

For other sources of ski information, call **Santa Fe Central Reservations** (tel. 505/983–8200; 800/776–7669 outside New Mexico), or **Ski New Mexico** (tel. 505/982–5300 or 800/755–7669) for general information about downhill or cross-country skiing conditions around Santa Fe.

Tennis

Santa Fe has more than two dozen public tennis courts available on a first-come, first-served basis. For information about the public facilities listed below and additional ones, call the **City Parks Division** (tel. 505/473–7236).

There are four asphalt courts at **Alto Park** (1035½ Alto St.). **Herb Martínez/La Resolana Park** (Camino Carlos Rey) has four concrete courts. **Ortíz Park** (Camino de las Crucitas) has three asphalt courts. There are two asphalt courts at **Fort Marcy Complex** (490 Washington Ave.).

Among the major private tennis facilities, including indoor, outdoor, and lighted courts, are **Club at El Gancho** (Old Las Vegas Hwy., tel. 505/988–5000), **Sangre De Cristo Racquet Club** (1755 Camino Corrales, tel. 505/983–7978), **Santa Fe Country Club** (Airport Rd., tel. 505/471–3378), and **Shellaberger Tennis Center** (College of Santa Fe, St. Michael's Dr., tel. 505/473–6144).

Windsurfing

Strong summer breezes and a proximity to man-made lakes have made northern New Mexico a popular windsurfing spot, though the water can be chilly and the winds unpredictable. Early morning is the best time to go, because thunderstorms often develop in the afternoon. Devoted regulars head to **Abiquiú Lake** (U.S. 84/285, Abiquiú, tel. 505/685–4371), 40 mi northwest of Santa Fe and backed by sculptural red-rock cliffs. **Cochiti Lake** (I–25, Santo Domingo Exit, Peña Blanca, tel. 505/242–8302) lies between Los Alamos and Santa Fe.

NIGHTLIFE AND THE ARTS

Santa Fe is perhaps America's most cultured small city. Gallery openings, poetry readings, plays, and dance concerts take place year-round, not to mention the famed opera and chamber-music festivals. Check the arts and entertainment listings in Santa Fe's daily newspaper, the *New Mexican*, particularly on Friday, when the arts and entertainment section, *Pasatiempo*, is included, or check the weekly *Santa Fe Reporter* for shows and events. Activities peak in the summer.

NIGHTLIFE

A handful of bars have spirited entertainment, from flamenco dancing to smokin' bands. Austin-based blues and country groups and other acts wander into town, and members of blockbuster bands have been known to perform unannounced at small clubs while vacationing in the area. But on most nights your best bet might be quiet cocktails beside the flickering embers of a piñon fire or under the stars out on the patio. Mellow entertainers perform nightly in many hotel bars. There is always one nightclub in town hosting rock-and-roll, swing, or Latin music.

Catamount Bar (125 E. Water St., tel. 505/988–7222) is popular with the post-college set; jazz and blues/rock groups play on weekends and some weeknights. The dance floor isn't great—too small, and with bright lights.

Club Alegría (Agua Fria Rd., just south of Siler Rd., tel. 505/471–2324) is the venue for Friday-night salsa dance parties. Father Frank Pretto, known as the Salsa Priest (a genuine Catholic priest), and his very hot salsa band, Pretto and Parranda, pour out salsa, boleros, rhumba, and merengue in the mirrored dance hall–bar. Security is in force, and the crowd is friendly, so don't be intimidated by the location. Free dance lessons start at 8. Blues, Mexican songs, and oldies are performed other nights of the week.

Dragon Room (406 Old Santa Fe Trail, tel. 505/983–7712) at the Pink Adobe restaurant has been the place to see and be seen in Santa Fe for decades; flamenco and other light musical acts entertain at the packed bar.

Eldorado Hotel (309 W. San Francisco St., tel. 505/988–4455) has a gracious lobby lounge where classical guitarists and pianists perform nightly.

El Farol (808 Canyon Rd., tel. 505/983–9912) restaurant is where locals like to hang out in an old Spanish-Western atmosphere and listen to flamenco, country, folk, and blues. Dancers pack the floor on weekend nights in summer.

Evangelo's (200 W. San Francisco St., tel. 505/982–9014) is an old-fashioned, smoky street-side bar, with pool tables, 200 types of imported beer, and rock bands on many weekends.

Paramount (331 Sandoval St., tel. 505/982–8999) has a snappy theme for each night of the week. The interior is contemporary and well lit and the dance floor is large. It's a good place to meet people, especially on swing night, when all ages over 21 swing, jitterbug, and lindy. There's also a Latin dance night, trash disco, and on Fridays, live music. Cover charge varies.

Rodeo Nites (2911 Cerrillos Rd., tel. 505/473–4138) attracts a country-western crowd. It can get a bit rough in the wee hours, so get there on the early side for line dancing and some very hot two-stepping.

THE ARTS

The performing arts scene in Santa Fe comes to life in the summer. Classical or jazz concerts, Shakespeare on the grounds of St. John's campus, experimental theater at Santa Fe Stages, or flamenco—"too many choices!" is the biggest complaint. The rest of the year is rather quiet, with seasonal music and dance performances. These events often double as benefits for nonprofit organizations and manage to bring top names to town. The historic Lensic Theater, Santa Fe's first and only movie palace from the 1930s, is being renovated into an 830-seat performing arts center. The Lensic Performing Arts Center is slated to open in spring of 2001.

Film

Cinematheque (1050 Old Pecos Trail, tel. 505/982–1338) screens foreign and independent films.

Music

The acclaimed **Santa Fe Chamber Music Festival** (Museum of Fine Arts, 107 E Palace Ave., tel. 505/983–2075) presents a

March Spring Music minifest and, in July and August, performances every night except Tuesday at the St. Francis Auditorium.

Santa Fe Opera (tel. 505/986–5900 or 800/280–4654, www.santafeopera.org) performs in a strikingly modern structure—a 2,126-seat, indoor-outdoor amphitheater with excellent acoustics and sight lines. Carved into the natural curves of a hillside 7 mi north of the city on U.S. 84/285, the opera overlooks mountains, mesas, and sky. Add some of the most acclaimed singers, directors, conductors, musicians, designers, and composers from Europe and the United States, and you begin to understand the excitement that builds every June. Richard Gaddes replaced founding director John Crosby in 2000, but no big changes are planned for the company, which presents five works in repertory each summer—a blend of seasoned classics, neglected masterpieces, and world premieres. Many evenings sell out far in advance, but inexpensive standing-room tickets are often available on the day of the performance.

The **Santa Fe Symphony** (tel. 505/983–3530 or 800/480–1319, www.sf_symphony.org) performs eight concerts each season (from September to May) and three concerts in the summer. In 2001 performances move to the **Lensic Performing Arts Center** (1050 Old Pecos Trail).

Orchestra and chamber concerts are given by the **Santa Fe Pro Musica** (tel. 505/988–4640) from September through April. Baroque and other classical compositions are the normal fare; the annual Christmas and April's Bach Festival performances are highlights.

Santa Fe Summerscene (tel. 505/438–8834) presents free concerts (rhythm and blues, light opera, jazz, Cajun, salsa, folk, and bluegrass) and dance performances (modern, folk) in the Santa Fe Plaza every Tuesday and Thursday from mid-June to August at noon and 6 PM.

On the campus of the Santa Fe Indian School, the **Paolo Soleri Outdoor Amphitheater** (1501 Cerrillos Rd., tel. 505/982–1889) hosts summer concert series.

Theater

The **Greer Garson Theater** (College of Santa Fe, 1600 St. Michael's Dr., tel. 505/473–6511, www.csf.edu) stages student productions of comedies, dramas, and musicals from October to May.

The **Santa Fe Community Theatre** (142 East De Vargas St., tel. 505/988–4262) has been presenting an adventurous mix of avant-garde pieces, classical drama, and musical comedy since 1922. The Fiesta Melodrama, which started in the 1920s—a spoof of the Santa Fe scene—takes place during September's Fiestas de Santa Fe.

Santa Fe Stages (100 N. Guadalupe, tel. 505/982–6683), an international theater festival, produces and presents professional theater, dance, and music from late June to August.

On Fridays, Saturdays, and Sundays during July and August, **Shakespeare in Santa Fe** (tel. 505/982–2910) presents performances of the Bard's finest in the courtyard of the John Gaw Meem Library at St. John's College (1160 Camino Cruz Blanca). A performance of Renaissance music begins at 6, followed by the play at 7:30. Seating is limited to 350, so it's best to get tickets in advance. Bring a picnic basket or buy food at the concession stand. It can get cold and the performers have been known to keep the show going in light rain. Tickets cost between $10 and $28. Grass seating is free, though a $5 donation is suggested. There are also several matinees during the season.

WHERE TO STAY

In Santa Fe, you can ensconce yourself in quintessential Santa Fe style or anonymous hotel-chain decor, depending on how much

santa fe lodging

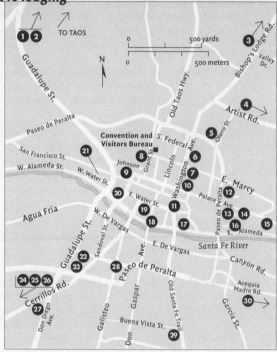

TO TAOS

500 yards
500 meters

N

Guadalupe St.

Bishop's Lodge Rd.

Valley Dr.

Artist Rd.

Old Taos Hwy.

Paseo de Peralta

Otero St.

San Francisco St.

Convention and Visitors Bureau

S. Federal

Johnson

Grant St.

Lincoln

Washington

W. Alameda St.

W. Water St.

E. Marcy

Palace Ave.

E. Water St.

Paseo de Peralta

Agua Fria

W. De Vargas

E. Alameda

Guadalupe St.

Sandoval St.

E. De Vargas

Santa Fe River

Paseo de Peralta

Canyon Rd.

Acequia Madre Rd.

Cerrillos Rd.

Gaspar

Old Santa Fe Trail

Garcia St.

Don Diego Ave.

Gallisteo

Buena Vista St.

Don

you want to spend. Cheaper motels and hotels are on Cerrillos (pronounced sah-*ree*-yos) Road—Santa Fe's strip of could-be-anywhere fast-food and lodging chains. Enchantment and prices rise the closer you get to the Plaza. There are also many bed-and-breakfasts and campgrounds. Even if you are 5 mi from the Plaza, getting around is easy by bus or car. Rates become lower in the off-season, from November to April (excluding Thanksgiving and Christmas). For price categories, *see* the chart *under* Lodging *in* Practical Information.

DOWNTOWN SANTA FE

$$$$ CAMPANILLA COMPOUND. If you want to feel like a Santa Fean living on prime, downtown real estate, stay at this private, tastefully decorated compound. Each unit has its own small courtyard with barbecue grill, landscaping, wood or tile floors, high ceilings, fabulous light, and a fireplace. It's ideal for families and groups—there's a full kitchen and a washer and dryer. Each one-bedroom unit sleeps up to four people, two-bedroom units up to six. This privacy and spaciousness is a pleasant five-block walk from the Plaza. There's a two-night minimum stay, and a $50 cleaning fee is added to the room charge. *334 Otero St., 87501, tel. 505/988–7585 or 800/828–9700. 15 units. Outdoor hot tub. AE, MC, V.*

$$$$ ELDORADO HOTEL. The city's largest hotel, a too-modern affair for some, is in the heart of downtown, close to the Plaza. Rooms are stylishly furnished with carved Southwestern-style desks and chairs, large upholstered club chairs, and art prints. Many rooms have terraces or kiva-style fireplaces. Baths are spacious and completely tiled. The Old House restaurant (☞ Eating Out, *above*) is highly rated. There's music nightly, from classical Spanish guitar to piano, in the comfortable lobby lounge. *309 W. San Francisco St., 87501, tel. 505/988–4455 or 800/955–4455, fax 505/995–4543. 201 rooms, 18 suites, 55 casitas, 8 condos. 2 restaurants, bar, lounge, pool, hot tub, sauna, health club, shops, concierge, convention*

center, meeting rooms, parking (fee). AE, D, DC, MC, V.
www.eldoradohotel.com

$$$$ HILTON OF SANTA FE. While this hotel claims to offer a Santa Fe experience, once you leave the lobby, which displays tasteful Santa Fe style, most of the rooms look like anywhere U.S.A. You'll get predictable, dependable Hilton service, but not much imagination or magic. *100 Sandoval St., 87501, tel. 505/988–2811 or 800/221–2424, fax 505/986–6435. 157 rooms. Restaurant, bar, lounge, pool, hot tub, concierge, parking (fee). AE, D, DC, MC, V.* www.hiltonsantafe.com

$$$$ HOTEL LORETTO. Formerly known as the Inn at Loretto, the Pueblo-style hotel attracts a loyal clientele year after year, many of whom swear by the friendly, outstanding service they receive. The lobby opens up to the gardens and pool, and leather couches and high-end architectural details make the hotel a pleasure to relax in. The restaurant, Nellie's, serves new American cuisine with plenty of meats and seafood. Next door is the Loretto Chapel. *211 Old Santa Fe Trail, 87501, tel. 505/988–5531, 800/727–5531 outside NM; fax 505/984–7988. 140 rooms, 5 suites. Restaurant, lounge, pool, shops. AE, D, DC, MC, V.* www.hotelloretto.com

$$$$ HOTEL SANTA FE. Picurís Pueblo maintains the controlling interest in this Pueblo-style three-story hotel. Rooms and suites are done in traditional Southwestern style, with locally handmade furniture, wooden blinds, and Pueblo paintings (*Picurís* means "those who paint"), many by Gerald Nailor. The hotel gift shop, the only tribally owned store in Santa Fe, has lower prices than many nearby retail stores. The Corn Dance Cafe serves Native American cuisine with a nouvelle twist. Guests can learn about Native American history and culture from informal talks held in the lobby by Alan Osbourne, an extremely well versed scholar. Native American dances take place May through October. *1501 Paseo de Peralta, 87505, tel. 505/982–1200, 800/825–9876 outside NM; fax 505/ 983–0785. 40 rooms, 91 suites. Restaurant, pool, outdoor hot tub. AE, D, DC, MC, V.* www.hotelsantafe.com

$$$$ ★ **INN OF THE ANASAZI.** In the heart of downtown, this hotel is one of Santa Fe's finest, with superb craftsmanship in every architectural detail. Each room has a beamed ceiling, kiva-style fireplace, and handcrafted furniture. Amenities include attentive concierge services, twice-daily maid service, room delivery of exercise bikes upon request, and a library with books on New Mexico and the Southwest. The Anasazi restaurant (☞ Eating Out, *above*) serves contemporary cuisine with uniquely regional accents. *113 Washington Ave., 87501, tel. 505/988–3030 or 800/688–8100, fax 505/988–3277. 59 rooms. Restaurant, in-room safes, minibars, in-room VCRs. AE, D, DC, MC, V. www.innoftheanasazi.com*

$$$$ **INN OF THE GOVERNORS.** The intimate lobby and gracious service at this hotel two blocks from the Plaza will quickly make you feel at home. The standard rooms have a Mexican theme, with bright colors, hand-painted folk art, Southwestern fabrics, and handmade furnishings; deluxe rooms also have balconies and fireplaces. New Mexican dishes and lighter fare like wood-oven pizzas are served in the dining room. *234 Don Gaspar Ave., 87501, tel. 505/982–4333 or 800/234–4534, fax 505/989–9149. 100 rooms. Dining room, piano bar, pool, free parking. AE, D, DC, MC, V. www.innofthegovernors.com*

$$$$ **INN ON THE ALAMEDA.** Between the Plaza and Canyon Road is one of the city's best small hotels. Alameda means "tree-lined lane," and this one perfectly complements the inn's riverside location. The adobe architecture and enclosed courtyards combine a relaxed New Mexico country atmosphere with the luxury and amenities of a top-notch hotel. Rooms have a Southwestern color scheme, handmade armoires and headboards, and ceramic lamps and tiles. *303 E. Alameda St., 87501, tel. 505/984–2121 or 800/289–2122, fax 505/986–8325. 59 rooms, 10 suites. Bar, refrigerators, 2 hot tubs, exercise room. AE, D, DC, MC, V. CP. www.inn-alameda.com*

$$$$ **LA FONDA.** A rich history and charm are more prevalent in this sole Plaza-front hotel than first-class service and amenities. The present structure, built in 1922 and enlarged many times, captures the essence of authentic Santa Fe style——the Pueblo-inspired architecture that defines the town today. Antiques and Native American art decorate the tiled lobby, and each room has hand-decorated wood furniture, wrought-iron light fixtures, and beamed ceilings. Some of the suites have fireplaces. There are 14 rooms for environmentally sensitive guests. La Plazuela Restaurant, with its hand-painted glass tiles, is a joy to sit in, but the food is disappointing. Folk and Latin jazz bands rotate nightly in the bar. *100 E. San Francisco St., 87501, tel. 505/982–5511, 800/523–5002 outside NM; fax 505/988–2952. 143 rooms, 24 suites. Restaurant, bar, pool, 2 hot tubs, massage, meeting rooms, parking (fee). AE, D, DC, MC, V. www.lafondasantfe.com*

$$$$ LA POSADA DE SANTA FE RESORT AND SPA. In 1999 new owners undertook a massive renovation, transforming the *Posada* (shelter) into an upscale, valet-parking-only hotel. Unfortunately, gone are the gardens that once made this an oasis from the rest of downtown, but there is a bellhop around every corner. The decor is stunning—many rooms have fireplaces, beamed ceilings, and Native American rugs. The restaurant Fuego specializes in rotisserie dishes from around the world. The resort and spa amenities are supported by on-site body treatment staff. *330 E. Palace Ave., 87501, tel. 505/986–0000 or 800/727–5276, fax 505/982–6850. 120 rooms, 38 suites. Restaurant, bar, pool, spa, parking (fee). AE, D, DC, MC, V. www.laposadadesantafe.com*

$$$$ TERRITORIAL INN. Creature comforts are a high priority at this 1890s brick structure, set back off a busy downtown street two blocks from the Plaza. The well-maintained rooms have Victorian decor; No. 9 has a canopy bed and a fireplace. Afternoon treats and brandy-and-cookie nightcaps are among the extras. *215 Washington Ave., 87501, tel. 505/989–7737, fax 505/984–8682. 10 rooms, 8 with bath, 2 with shared bath. Hot tub, free parking. AE, DC, MC, V. CP. www.territorialinn.com*

$$$$ WATER STREET INN. The large rooms in this restored adobe 2½ ★ blocks from the Plaza are decorated with reed shutters, antique pine beds, hand-stenciled artwork, and a blend of cowboy, Hispanic, and Native American art and artifacts. Most have fireplaces; all have private baths, VCRs, cable TV, and voice mail. Afternoon hors d'oeuvres are served in the living room. A patio deck is available for relaxing. *427 W. Water St., 87501, tel. 505/ 984–1193 or 800/646–6752. 12 rooms. In-room VCRs, outdoor hot tub, free parking. AE, DC, MC, V. CP. www.waterstreetinn.com*

$$$–$$$$ **GRANT CORNER INN.** Though this B&B is downtown, the surrounding small garden and Victorian porch shaded by a huge weeping willow make it feel private. Antique Spanish and American country furnishings share space with potted greens and knickknacks. Room accents include old-fashioned fixtures, quilts, and Native American blankets. The ample breakfast, which is open to the public, includes home-baked breads and pastries, jellies, and blue-corn waffles. A separate hacienda, located six blocks north, can accommodate groups of up to seven people. It is connected via intercom to the inn, and guests are entitled to all of the inn's amenities, including free parking at the downtown location. *122 Grant Ave., 87501, tel. 505/983–6678, fax 505/983–1526. 8 rooms, 2 rooms in hacienda. Breakfast room, free parking. DC, MC, V. BP. www.grantcornerinn.com*

$$–$$$$ **ALEXANDER'S INN.** This two-story 1903 Craftsman-style house in
★ the Eastside residential area, a few blocks from the Plaza and Canyon Road, exudes the charm of an old country inn. Rooms have American country–style wooden furnishings and flower arrangements. There are also two two-story cottages with kitchens—perfect for groups (☞ The Madeleine, *below*). *529 E. Palace Ave., 87501, tel. 505/986–1431. 5 rooms, 2 with shared bath; 2 cottages. Outdoor hot tub. D, DC, MC, V. CP. www.collectorsguide.com/ alexandinn.com*

$$–$$$$ **INN OF THE TURQUOISE BEAR.** In the 1920s, poet Witter Bynner played host to an eccentric circle of artists and intellectuals, as well as some wild parties, in this mid-19th-century adobe home. The rooms in the rambling B&B are simple—no oversize televisions or big hotel trimmings, but there's plenty of ambience and a ranchlike lobby where you can stretch out or converse with other guests. You might sleep in the room where D. H. Lawrence and Frieda slept, or perhaps Robert Oppenheimer's room. The terraced flower gardens have plenty of places to repose, away from the traffic on Old Santa Fe Trail, which borders the property. *342 E. Buena Vista, 87504, tel. 505/983–0798 or 800/396–4104. 8 rooms, 2 with shared bath; 2 suites. AE, D, MC, V. CP. www.turquoisebear.com*

$$–$$$$ **THE MADELEINE.** Carolyn Lee, who owns Alexander's Inn (☞ *above*), has named her successful establishments after her children. The Madeleine is the only Queen Anne house in the city, three blocks east of the Plaza in a quiet garden setting. The public rooms are open, sunny, and genuine Queen Anne style, with fruit bowls, original and fantastically futuristic stained-glass windows, lace curtains, and fresh-cut flowers. You'll feel as if you've made a genteel step back in time. Rooms in the main home are furnished in ornate late-19th-century fashion. *106 Faithway St., 87501, tel. 505/982–3465 or 888/321–5123, fax 505/982–8572. 6 rooms, 2 cottages. AE, D, MC, V. BP. www.madeleine.com*

$$$ **DUNSHEE'S.** So romantic that its patio has been used for weddings, this B&B is in the quiet Eastside area, a mile from the Plaza, where the oldest stone irrigation ditch still runs with water in spring and summer. Acequia Madre (Mother Ditch) is one of the oldest and most enchanting roads in Santa Fe (it runs parallel to Canyon Road). The suite is the restored adobe home of artist Susan Dunshee, the proprietor; the adobe casita is good for families. The suite has a living room, a bedroom with a queen bed, kiva-style fireplaces, and viga ceilings, and is decorated with antiques and works by area artists. The casita has two bedrooms, a living room, a patio, a completely equipped and stocked kitchen, and a kiva-style fireplace, and is adorned with decorative linens and folk art. *986 Acequia Madre, 87501, tel. 505/982–0988. 1 suite, 1 small house. MC, V. BP in suite, CP in casita. www.bbhost.com/dunshees*

$$$ PUEBLO BONITO B&B INN. Rooms in this adobe compound built in 1873 have handmade and hand-painted furnishings, Navajo weavings, sand paintings and pottery, locally carved *santos* (saints), and Western art. All have kiva fireplaces, and many have kitchens. Breakfast is served in the main dining room. Afternoon tea also offers complimentary margaritas. The Plaza is a five-minute walk away. *138 W. Manhattan Ave., 87501, tel. 505/984–8001 or 800/461–4599, fax 505/984–3155. 11 rooms, 7 suites. Dining room, hot tub, coin laundry. AE, DC, MC, V. CP. www.pueblobonito.com*

$$$ RADISSON HOTEL & SUITES ON THE PLAZA, SANTA FE. The rooms at the handsome, brick-trimmed, Territorial-style hotel, formerly the Plaza Real, have maintained their charm, despite incorporation into a large chain. All rooms are off an interior brick courtyard. Handcrafted Southwestern furniture decorates the large rooms, and most have patios or balconies and wood-burning fireplaces. *125 Washington Ave., 87501, tel. 505/988–4900 or 800/537–8483, fax 505/983–9322. 13 rooms, 43 suites. Breakfast room, lounge. AE, D, DC, MC, V. www.radisson.com*

$$–$$$ INN OF THE ANIMAL TRACKS. This restored Pueblo-style home three blocks east of the Plaza has beamed ceilings, hardwood floors, handcrafted furniture, and fireplaces. Each guest room is decorated with an animal theme, such as Soaring Eagle or Gentle Deer. On the cutesy side, the Whimsical Rabbit Room is filled with stuffed and terra-cotta rabbit statues, rabbit books, rabbit drawings. Bunny-rabbit slippers are under the bed. (This room opens directly onto the kitchen, where the cook arrives at 6 AM.) The backyard is delightful. The inn is on the curve of a busy road that loops around the historic center of town—somewhat noisy, but ideal for access to both the Plaza and Canyon Road. *707 Paseo de Peralta, 87504, tel. 505/988–1546, fax 505/982–8098. 5 rooms. AE, MC, V. BP.*

$$–$$$ ST. FRANCIS. Listed in the National Register of Historic Places, this three-story building, parts of which were constructed in 1920, has walkways lined with turn-of-the-20th-century lampposts and is just one block south of the Plaza. The simple and elegant rooms with high ceilings, casement windows, brass-and-iron beds, marble and cherry antiques, and original artworks suggest a refined establishment, but the service has been known to fall short. Afternoon tea, with scones and finger sandwiches, is served daily (not complimentary) in the huge lobby, which rises 50 ft from a floor of blood-red tiles. The St. Francis Club, which has a very English feel, serves Continental fare. The hotel bar is among the few places in town where you can grab a bite to eat until midnight. *210 Don Gaspar Ave., 87501, tel. 505/983–5700 or 800/529–5700, fax 505/989–7690. 83 rooms. Restaurant, bar, free parking. AE, D, DC, MC, V. www.hotelstfrancis.com*

CERRILLOS ROAD

$$ EL REY INN. The tree-shaded, whitewashed El Rey has been a Santa Fe landmark motel for 65 years. Rooms are decorated in Southwestern, Spanish colonial, and Victorian styles. Some have kitchenettes and fireplaces. The largest suite, with seven rooms, sleeps six and has antique furniture, a full kitchen, a breakfast nook, and two patios. Service is friendly. *1862 Cerrillos Rd., 87501, tel. 505/982–1931 or 800/521–1349, fax 505/989–9249. 79 rooms, 8 suites. Kitchenettes, pool, 2 hot tubs, sauna, playground, coin laundry. AE, DC, MC, V. CP.*

$$ SANTA FE BUDGET INN. On the southern edge of the Railyard District, this inn offers affordable comfort and standard Southwestern decor within walking distance of the Plaza (six blocks). Special packages are available for three- and four-day stays during peak-season events such as Indian Market. Full breakfast is complimentary during off-season. *725 Cerrillos Rd., 87501, tel. 505/982–5952, fax 505/984–8879. 160 rooms. 2 restaurants, pool. AE, DC, MC, V. CP. www.elreyinnsantafe.com*

$$ SANTA FE MOTEL. Walking-distance proximity to the Plaza is a prime asset of this property—an unusually successful upgrade of a standard motel. Rooms, some with kitchenettes, are decorated in contemporary Southwestern style. *510 Cerrillos Rd., 87501, tel. 505/982–1039 or 800/999–1039, fax 505/986–1275. 13 rooms, 8 casitas. Kitchenettes (some). AE, D, MC, V. www.santafemotelinn.com*

$ MOTEL 6. The amenities at this well-maintained chain property several miles from the Plaza include an outdoor pool, free HBO, and free local calls. Those under 17 stay free with their parents. *3007 Cerrillos Rd., 87505, tel. 505/473–1380, fax 505/473–7784. 104 rooms. Pool. AE, DC, MC, V.*

$ SILVER SADDLE MOTEL. If you want a taste of late 1950s Western kitsch, try this motel, built when Cerrillos Road was the main route to Albuquerque and the village of Cerrillos. Some of the rooms have kitchenettes and adjoining open carports: nothing fancy, but very nostalgic. It's next door to the Mexican-style market Jackalope, which has a café. *2810 Cerrillos Rd., 87505, tel. 505/471–7663, fax 505/471–1066. 27 rooms with bath or shower. Kitchenettes (some). DC, MC, V. www.motelsantafe.com*

NORTH OF SANTA FE

$$$$ BISHOP'S LODGE. This resort established in 1918 is in a bucolic
★ valley at the foot of the Sangre de Cristo Mountains and yet only a five-minute drive from the Plaza. Behind the main building is an exquisite chapel that was once the private retreat of Archbishop Jean Baptiste Lamy. Outdoor activities include horseback riding, organized trail riding (with meals) into the adjacent national forest, skeet-shooting, and trapshooting. At press time, indoor exercise facilities were being expanded and rooms added. The two lodge buildings have antique Southwestern furnishings—shipping chests, tinwork from Mexico, and Native American and Western art. The restaurant serves a Continental menu with a Southwestern touch. A bountiful brunch, probably the best in Santa Fe, is served on Sunday. *Bishop's Lodge Rd., 2½ mi north of downtown, 87501, tel.*

505/983–6377 or 800/732–2240, fax 505/989–8739. 70 rooms, 18 suites. Restaurant, bar, pool, hot tub, spa, 4 tennis courts, exercise room, hiking, horseback riding, fishing, airport shuttle. AE, D, MC, V. www.bishopslodge.com

$$$$ ★ HACIENDA DEL CEREZO. Stop reading here if $600 is more than you want to spend on a room. Keep in mind that the rate includes three meals for two people prepared by a master chef; dinner is a five-course candlelit affair in the great room or in the courtyard, looking out onto the vanishing-edge pool and the desert beyond. The inn sits on a splendidly isolated patch of land 25 minutes northwest of downtown. Rooms are subtly executed in prints, ornaments, carvings on the beams of the viga ceilings, and etchings in the glass shower doors. Each room has a king-size bed, a generous sitting area, a kiva fireplace, an enclosed patio, and a view of the mountains. Service is gracious and understated. 100 Camino del Cerezo, 87501, tel. 505/982–8000 or 888/982–8001, fax 505/983–7162. 10 rooms. Dining room, pool, outdoor hot tub, tennis court, hiking, horseback riding. AE. FAP.

$$$$ ★ RANCHO ENCANTADO. Robert Redford, Johnny Cash, Robert Plant, and the Dalai Lama are among the past guests of this resort on 168 acres. The accommodations have Southwestern-style furniture, handmade and hand-painted, in addition to fine Spanish and Western pieces from the 1850s and earlier. Some of the villas and rooms have fireplaces, private patios, and tiled floors; others have carpeting and refrigerators. The dining room, with a terrific view of the Jemez Mountains, serves good Continental fare. 198 State Rd. 592, 8 mi north of Santa Fe off U.S. 84/285 near Tesuque, 87501, tel. 505/982–3537 or 800/722–9339, fax 505/983–8269. 29 rooms, 22 villas. Dining room, pool, outdoor hot tub, 2 tennis courts, hiking. AE, D, DC, MC, V. www.ranchoencantadosantafe.com

$$$–$$$$ TEN THOUSAND WAVES/HOUSES OF THE MOON. The Zenlike atmosphere of this Japanese-style health spa and resort above town offers an East-meets-West retreat for adults. Eight small hillside houses are reached by a path through the piñons. All have brick floors, marble fireplaces, fine woodwork, futon beds, and adobe-color walls; two come with full kitchens. The ambience is suited toward organic rather than antiseptic tastes. The facility has private and communal indoor and outdoor hot tubs and spa treatments. Tubs run from $19 to $26 per hour; massage and spa treatments cost from $35 to $120. Overnight guests can use the communal mens's and women's hot tubs free of charge. The health bar serves sushi. *Box 10200, 87504, 4 mi from the Plaza on road to Santa Fe Ski Basin, tel. 505/982–9304, fax 505/989–5077. 8 cabins. 9 outdoor hot tubs, massage, spa, gift shop, snack bar. D, MC, V. www.tenthousandwaves.com*

CAMPGROUNDS

The Santa Fe National Forest is right in the city's backyard and includes the Dome Wilderness (5,200 acres in the volcanically formed Jemez Mountains) and the Pecos Wilderness (223,333 acres of high mountains, forests, and meadows at the southern end of the Rocky Mountain chain). Public campsites are open from May to October, and all the ones listed here have hot showers.

For a report on general conditions, call the **Santa Fe National Forest Office** (1220 S. St. Francis Dr. [Box 1689], 87504, tel. 505/438–7840). For a one-stop shop for information about public lands, which includes national and state parks, contact the **New Mexico Public Lands Information Center** (1474 Rodeo Rd. 87505, tel. 505/438–7542, fax 505/438–7582, www.publiclands.org) on the south side of Santa Fe. It has maps, reference materials, licenses, permits—just about everything you need to plan a trip into the New Mexican wilderness.

⚠ **Babbitt's Los Campos RV Resort.** The only full-service RV park within the city limits, Los Campos even has a swimming pool. There's a car dealership on one side and open vistas on the other: poplars and Russian olive trees, a dry riverbed, and

Your checklist for a perfect journey

WAY AHEAD

- Devise a trip budget.
- Write down the five things you want most from this trip. Keep this list handy before and during your trip.
- Make plane or train reservations. Book lodging and rental cars.
- Arrange for pet care.
- Check your passport. Apply for a new one if necessary.
- Photocopy important documents and store in a safe place.

A MONTH BEFORE

- Make restaurant reservations and buy theater and concert tickets. Visit fodors.com for links to local events.
- Familiarize yourself with the local language or lingo.

TWO WEEKS BEFORE

- Replenish your supply of medications.
- Create your itinerary.
- Enjoy a book or movie set in your destination to get you in the mood.

- Develop a packing list. Shop for missing essentials. Repair and launder or dry-clean your clothes.

A WEEK BEFORE

- Stop newspaper deliveries. Pay bills.
- Acquire traveler's checks.
- Stock up on film.
- Label your luggage.
- Finalize your packing list— take less than you think you need.
- Create a toiletries kit filled with travel-size essentials.
- Get lots of sleep. Don't get sick before your trip.

A DAY BEFORE

- Drink plenty of water.
- Check your travel documents.
- Get packing!

DURING YOUR TRIP

- Keep a journal/scrapbook.
- Spend time with locals.
- Take time to explore. Don't plan too much.

mountains rise in the background. The fee per night is $25. 3574 Cerrillos Rd., 87505, tel. 505/473–1949. 94 RV sites. Rest rooms, showers, pool. MC, V.

⚠ **Rancheros de Santa Fe Campground.** This camping park is on a hill in the midst of a piñon forest. You can get LP gas service here. Tent sites are $16.95, water and electric hookups $20.95, full hookups $23.95–$24.95, and cabins $31.95. On I–25N, Old Las Vegas Hwy. (Exit 290 on the Las Vegas Hwy., 10½ mi from the Plaza), 87505, tel. 505/466–3482. 95 RV sites, 37 tent sites. Rest rooms, showers, grocery, pool, coin laundry. MC, V. Nov.–Feb. 28.

⚠ **Santa Fe KOA.** In the foothills of the Sangre de Cristo Mountains, 20 minutes southeast of Santa Fe, this large campground is covered with piñons, cedars, and junipers. Tent sites are $17.95, water and electric hookups $21.95, full hookups $23.95, and cabins $31.95. Old Las Vegas Hwy. (NM 3), (Box 95-A), 87505, tel. 505/466–1419. 44 RV sites, 26 tent sites, 10 cabins. Rest rooms, showers, LP gas, grocery, recreation room, coin laundry. D, MC, V. Closed Nov.–Feb.

In This Chapter

Updated by Kathleen McCloud

side trips
from santa fe

ONE CAN HARDLY GRASP THE PROFUNDITY of New Mexico's ancient past or its immense landscape without journeying into the hinterland. Each of the excursions below can be accomplished in a day or less. The High Road to Taos is a very full day, so start early or plan on spending the night near Taos.

JEMEZ COUNTRY

In the Jemez region, the 1,000-year-old Anasazi ruins at Bandelier National Monument present a vivid contrast to Los Alamos National Laboratory, birthplace of the atomic bomb. You can easily take in part of Jemez Country in a day trip from Santa Fe; some of the sights beyond the end of the tour described below, among them Jemez Pueblo, are covered in Chapter 6. On the loop described you'll see terrific views of the Rio Grande Valley, the Sangre de Cristos, the Galisteo Basin, and, in the distance, the Sandias. There are places to eat and shop for essentials in Los Alamos and a few roadside diners in La Cueva, on the highway to Jemez Springs.

A fire in May 2000 burned much of the pine forest in the lower Jemez mountains. The once scenic drive is now scarred with charcoaled remains. Depending on fire hazard due to seasonal

76

droughts, access to New Mexico wilderness may be affected. A call to the New Mexico Public Lands Information Center (tel. 505/438–7582) is advisable when planning a trip.

Los Alamos

31 mi from Santa Fe, north on U.S. 84/285 (to Pojoaque) and west on NM 502.

The town of Los Alamos, a 45-minute drive from Santa Fe, was founded in absolute secrecy in 1943 as a center of war research, and its existence only became known in 1945 with the detonation of atomic bombs in Japan. The bomb was first tested in southern New Mexico, at White Sands Missile Range, but the think tank and laboratories that unleashed atomic power were firmly planted in the forested hillside of Los Alamos (*alamos* means "trees" in Spanish). Many of those trees burned in the May 2000 Cerro Grande fire, which destroyed the surrounding hillsides and burned 260 homes in Los Alamos. Reforestation is well under way. The topography will transform slowly, first with grasses. Aspen trees will be among the first trees to root, providing the conditions necessary for pine seedlings to come back.

In time, Los Alamos (referred to by Santa Feans as the "city on the hill," or, more recently, "L.A.,") will be green again, with stunning fall color in its aspen groves. The fire did not damage the business district. Architecturally, it continues to look and feel like a town that is utterly out of place in northern New Mexico. It's a fascinating place to visit because of the profound role it played in shaping the modern world.

The **Bradbury Science Museum** is Los Alamos National Laboratory's public showcase. You can experiment with lasers; use advanced computers; witness research in solar, geothermal, fission, and fusion energy; and view exhibits about World War II's Project Y (the Manhattan Project, whose participants developed the atomic bomb). *Los Alamos National Laboratory,*

15th St. and Central Ave., tel. 505/667–4444. Free. Tues.–Fri. 9–5, Sat.–Mon. 1–5.

The New Mexican architect John Gaw Meem designed the **Fuller Lodge,** a short drive up Central Avenue from the Bradbury Science Museum. The massive log building was erected in 1928 as a dining and recreation hall for a small private boys' school. In 1942 the federal government purchased the school and made it the base of operations for the Manhattan Project. Part of the lodge is an art center that shows the works of northern New Mexican artists. 2132 Central Ave., tel. 505/662–9331. Free. Mon.–Sat. 10–4.

The **Los Alamos Historical Museum,** in a log building adjoining Fuller Lodge, displays artifacts of early Native American life. Photographs and documents relate the community's history. 2132 Central Ave., tel. 505/662–4493. Free. Oct.–Apr., Mon.–Sat. 10–4, Sun. 1–4; May–Sept., Mon.–Sat. 9:30–4:30, Sun. 11–5.

EATING OUT

$–$$ HILL DINER. With a friendly staff and clientele, this large diner serves some of the finest burgers in town, along with chicken-fried steaks, homemade soups, and heaps of fresh vegetables. 1315 Trinity Dr., tel. 505/662–9745. AE, D, DC, MC, V.

WHERE TO STAY

$$ LOS ALAMOS INN. Rooms in this one-story hotel have modern Southwestern decor and sweeping canyon views. Ashley's, the inn's restaurant ($$) and bar, serves American and Southwestern regional specialties; the Sunday brunch is popular. 2201 Trinity Dr., 87544, tel. 505/662–7211, fax 505/661–7714. 115 rooms. Restaurant, bar, pool. AE, D, DC, MC, V.

$$ HILLTOP HOUSE HOTEL. Minutes from the Los Alamos National Laboratory, this hotel hosts both vacationers and scientists. All the rooms are furnished in modern Southwestern style; deluxe ones have kitchenettes. 400 Trinity Dr., at Central Ave. (Box 250), 87544, tel. 505/662–2441, fax 505/662–5913. 87 rooms, 13 suites. Restaurant,

lounge, indoor pool, exercise room, coin laundry. AE, D, DC, MC, V. CP.
www.vla.com/hilltophouse

$–$$ RENATA'S ORANGE STREET BED&BREAKFAST. Linda Hartman is
the new proprietor of this B&B. In an unremarkable 1948 wood-frame
house in a quiet residential neighborhood, rooms are furnished in
Southwestern and country style. The public area has cable TV and
a VCR, and you can use the kitchen and the laundry. *3496 Orange*
St., 87544, tel./fax 505/662–2651. 6 rooms, 2 with bath; 3 suites. AE, D,
DC, MC, V. BP. www.losalamos.com/organgestreetinn

Bandelier National Monument

40 mi from Santa Fe, north on U.S. 84/285, west on NM 502, south on
NM 501 (W. Jemez Rd.) to "T" intersection with NM 4; turn left (east)
and drive 6 mi to the monument's entrance.

Seven centuries before the Declaration of Independence was
signed, compact city-states existed in the Southwest. Remnants
of one of the most impressive of them can be seen at **Frijoles**
Canyon in Bandelier National Monument. At the canyon's base,
beside a gurgling stream, are the remains of cave dwellings,
ancient ceremonial kivas, and other stone structures that
stretch out for more than a mile beneath the sheer walls of the
canyon's tree-fringed rim. For hundreds of years the Anasazi
people, relatives of today's Rio Grande Pueblo Indians, thrived
on wild game, corn, and beans. Suddenly, for reasons still
undetermined, the settlements were abandoned.

Wander through the site on a paved, self-guided trail. If you can
climb primitive wooden ladders and squeeze through narrow
doorways, you can explore some of the cave dwellings and cell-
like rooms.

Bandelier National Monument, named after author and
ethnologist Adolph Bandelier (his novel *The Delight Makers* is set
in Frijoles Canyon), contains 23,000 acres of backcountry
wilderness, waterfalls, and wildlife. Sixty miles of trails traverse

the park. A small museum in the visitor center focuses on the area's prehistoric and contemporary Native American cultures, with displays of artifacts from 1200 to modern times. *tel. 505/ 672–3861. $10 per car, good for 7 days. Memorial Day–Labor Day, daily 8–6; Labor Day–Memorial Day, daily 8–5.*

Valle Grande

40 mi west of Santa Fe. From Bandelier National Monument, head west on NM 4 and follow the winding road through the mountain forest.

A high-forest drive brings you to the awe-inspiring Valle Grande, one of the world's largest calderas. You can't imagine the volcanic crater's immensity until you spot what look like specks of dust on the lush meadow floor and realize they're cows. The entire 50-mi Jemez range, formed by cataclysmic upheavals, is filled with streams, hiking trails, campgrounds, and hot springs—reminders of its volcanic origin. If you're coming from Bandelier National Monument (☞ *above*), the drive should take about 45 minutes. It's particularly pretty in late September or early October when the aspens turn gold.

THE HIGH ROAD TO TAOS

The main highway to Taos along the Rio Grande gorge (NM 68) provides dramatic close-ups of the river and rocky mountain faces, but if you have a couple of extra hours, the High Road to Taos provides sweeping views of woodlands and some traditional villages to explore. The High Road consists of U.S. 285 north to NM 503 (just past village of Pojoaque), to Santa Fe County Road 98 (a left at sign for Chimayó), to NM 76 northeast, to NM 75 east, to NM 518 north. The drive through the rolling foothills and tiny valleys of the Sangre de Cristos, dotted with orchards, pueblos, and picturesque villages, is stunning. In mid-April the orchards are in blossom; summer turns the valleys into lush green oases; and in fall, the smell of piñon adds to the sensual overload of golden leaves and red-chile ristras hanging from the houses. In winter, the fields are covered with quilts of snow, and the lines of homes, fences, and trees stand out like bold pen-and-ink drawings against the sky. But the roads can be icy and treacherous. If your rental car isn't up to adverse weather conditions, take the "low road" to Taos. If you decide to take the High Road just one way between Santa Fe and Taos, you might want to save it for the return journey—the scenery is best enjoyed when traveling north to south.

Española

20 mi from Santa Fe, north on U.S. 285/84.

Only a 20-minute drive north of Santa Fe is the Española Valley, where rivers and state highways converge to form the epicenter of the valley—Española. This is the land of '53 turquoise Chevy pick-ups and red TransAms that practically scrape the ground, chain steering wheels, tiny tires, and shiny hubcaps. Vying for attention with these low-riders are trucks hoisted 4 ft off the ground by oversize tires. A few miles north of Española on U.S. 285/84, the highway splits, 84 heading northwest through the Rio Chama valley, and 285 cutting east and then straight north toward Ojo Caliente (☞ *below*). Highway 68 heads northeast toward Taos. All of the main arteries converge in the heart of town in a confusing maze, so watch the signs on the south side of town. Tank up here before making a road trip north. Traffic moves slowly, especially on weekend nights when cruisers bring car culture alive. Both the Low Riders Club and the Hot Rod and Drag Racing Club have chapters in Española. More of a crossroads than a destination, Española has a few outstanding restaurants that serve northern New Mexican cuisine and are worth the trip.

EATING OUT

$$-$$$ EL PARAGUA RESTAURANT. With a dark, intimate atmosphere of wood and stone, this place offers a more formal ambience for New Mexican and Mexican cuisine. Steaks and fish are grilled over

a mesquite-wood fire. *603 Santa Cruz Rd. (*
505/753–3211 or 800/929–8226. D, MC, V.

$–$$ **JOANN'S RANCHO CASADOS.** JoAnn Cas
in Española, where she learned to grow
ranch still provides many of the fresh ingre
the great chiles rellenos, *posole (corn with pork in a*
enchiladas. Half portions and a children's menu are served as well.
The casual decor includes brightly striped Mexican blankets on
the walls. Beer and wine are served. *418 North Riverside Dr. (on Hwy.*
68), tel. 505/753–2837. Reservations not accepted. D, MC, V. Closed Sun.

Chimayó

25 mi north of Santa Fe, 7 mi east of Española on NM 76

From Santa Fe, you can take the scenic NM 503, which winds past
horses and orchards in the narrow Nambé Valley, then ascends
into the red-rock canyons with a view of Truchas Peaks to the
northeast before dropping into the bucolic village of Chimayó.
New Mexico's state motto, "The Land of Enchantment," is hard
to deny once you lay eyes on this village. It is not to be missed.
Nestled into hillsides where gnarled piñons seem to grow from
bare bedrock, Chimayó is famed for its weaving, its food, and its
two chapels.

The **Santuario de Chimayó,** a small frontier adobe church, has
a fantastically carved and painted wood altar and is built on the
site where, believers say, a mysterious light came from the
ground on Good Friday in 1810 and where a large wooden
crucifix was found beneath the earth. The chapel sits above a
sacred *pozito* (a small hole), the dirt from which is believed to
have miraculous healing properties. Dozens of abandoned
crutches and braces placed in the anteroom—along with many
notes, letters, and photos—testify to this. The Santuario draws
a steady stream of worshipers all year long—Chimayó is

onsidered the Lourdes of the Southwest. During Holy Week as many as 50,000 pilgrims come here. The shrine is a National Historic Landmark, but unlike similar holy places, this one is not inundated by commercialism; a few small adobe shops nearby sell religious articles, brochures, and books. Mass is celebrated on Sundays. *Off SF County Rd. 98, look for sign and turn right, tel. 505/351–4889. Free. Daily 9–5:30.*

A smaller chapel just 200 yards from El Santuario was built in 1857 and dedicated to **Santo Niño de Atocha.** As at the more famous Santuario, the dirt at Santo Niño de Atocha's chapel is said to have healing properties in the place where the *Santo Niño* was first placed. The little boy saint was brought here from Mexico by Severiano Medina, who claimed Santo Niño de Atocha had healed him of rheumatism. San Ildefonso pottery master Maria Martinez came here for healing as a child. Tales of the boy saint losing one of his shoes as he wandered through the countryside helping those in trouble endeared him to the people of northern New Mexico. It became a tradition to place shoes at the foot of the statue as an offering. *Free. Daily 9–5:30.*

EATING OUT

$$–$$$ RANCHO DE CHIMAYÓ. In a century-old adobe hacienda tucked into the mountains, with whitewashed walls, hand-stripped vigas, and cozy dining rooms, the Rancho de Chimayó is still owned and operated by the family that first occupied the house. There's a roaring fireplace in winter and, in summer, a terraced patio shaded by catalpa trees. You can take an after-dinner stroll on the grounds' paths. Reservations are essential in summer. *SF County Rd. 98, tel. 505/351–4444 or 505/984–2100. AE, D, DC, MC, V.*

$ LEONA'S DE CHIMAYÓ. This fast-food-style burrito and chile stand at one end of the Santuario de Chimayó parking lot has only a few tables, and in summer it's crowded. The specialty is flavored tortillas—everything from jalapeño to butterscotch. (Her business became so successful that owner Leona Tiede opened a tortilla factory in Chimayó's Manzana Center.) *Off SF County Rd. 98, behind*

Santuario de Chimayó, tel. 505/351–4569 or 888/561–5569. AE, D, DC, MC, V.

WHERE TO STAY

$$–$$$ **CASA ESCONDIDA.** Intimate and peaceful, this adobe inn has sweeping views of the Sangre de Cristo range. The setting makes it a great base for mountain bikers. Chopin on the CD player and the scent of fresh-baked strudel waft through the rooms; owner Irenka Taurek, who speaks several languages, and manager Matthew Higgi provide an international welcome. Rooms are decorated with antiques and Native American and other regional arts and crafts. Ask for the Sun Room, in the main house, which has a private patio, viga ceilings, and a brick floor. The separate one-bedroom Casita Escondida has a kiva-style fireplace, tile floors, kitchen, and a sitting area. A large hot tub is hidden in a grove behind wild berry bushes. *Off NM 76 at Mile Marker 0100 (Box 142), 85722*, tel. 505/351–4805 or 800/643–7201, fax 505/351–2575. *7 rooms, 1 house. Outdoor hot tub. AE, MC, V. BP. www.casaescondida.com*

$$ **HACIENDA DE CHIMAYÓ.** This authentic adobe house is furnished with antiques, and each room has a private bath and fireplace. The inn doesn't offer much in the way of seclusion since it's directly on Chimayó's main road, but it is conveniently across from the lovely Rancho de Chimayó restaurant and within walking distance of the Santuario. *Off SF County Rd. 98 (Box 11), Chimayo 87522*, tel. 505/351–2222 or 888/270–2320. *6 rooms, 1 suite. AE, MC, V. CP.*

$$ **LA POSADA DE CHIMAYÓ.** New Mexico's first B&B is a peaceful place whose two suites have fireplaces, Mexican rugs, handwoven bedspreads, and comfortable regional furniture. The entire guest house can be rented by the week and the minimum stay is two nights. Views are somewhat obscured and the house is set close to the dirt road. *279 Rio Arriba, County Rd. 0101 (Box 463), 87522*, tel./fax 505/351–4605. *2 suites. No credit cards. BP.*

SHOPPING

Centinela Traditional Arts-Weaving (NM 76, approximately 1 mi east of the junction with County Rd. 98, tel. 505/351–2180 or 877/351–2180) continues the Trujillo family weaving tradition, which started in northern New Mexico more than seven generations ago. Irvin Trujillo and his wife, Lisa, are both award-winning master weavers, creating Rio Grande–style tapestry blankets and rugs, many of them with natural dyes that authentically replicate early weavings. Most designs are historically based, but the Trujillos contribute their own designs as well. The shop and gallery carries these heirloom-quality textiles, with a knowledgeable staff on hand to demonstrate or answer questions about the weaving technique.

Ortega's Weaving Shop (NM 76 at County Rd. 98, look for the sign on the left if going north on SF County Rd. 98, tel. 505/351–4215 or 877/351–4215) sells Rio Grande– and Chimayó-style textiles made by the family whose Spanish ancestors brought the craft to New Mexico in the 1600s. The Galeria Ortega, next door, sells traditional New Mexican and Hispanic and contemporary Native American arts and crafts. The shop is closed on Sunday.

Cordova

28 mi north of Santa Fe. From Chimayó, go north on NM 76 for about 4 mi, turn right onto the road at Mountain View Elementary School.

Hardly more than a mountain village with a small central plaza, a school, a post office, and a church, Cordova is the center of the regional wood-carving industry. The town supports 35 full-time and part-time carvers. Most of them are descendants of José Dolores López, who in the 1920s created the village's signature unpainted "Cordova style" of carving. Most of the *santeros* (makers of religious images) have signs outside their homes indicating that santos are for sale. The pieces are expensive, ranging from several hundred dollars for small ones to several thousand for larger figures. There are also affordable and delightful small carvings of animals and birds. The **St. Anthony of Padua Chapel,** which is filled with handcrafted retablos and other religious art, is worth a visit.

Truchas

35 mi north of Santa Fe; from Cordova, take NM 76 1½ mi north.

Truchas (Spanish for "trout") is where Robert Redford shot the movie *The Milagro Beanfield War* (based on the much-better novel written by Taos author John Nichols). This village is perched on the rim of a deep canyon beneath the towering Truchas Peaks, mountains high enough to be almost perpetually capped with snow. The tallest of the Truchas Peaks is 13,102 ft, the second-highest point in New Mexico. There are a few galleries and a small market in this town, which feels like an outpost just waking up from the colonial days.

SHOPPING
The most notable of the colorful shops and galleries in Truchas is **Cordova's Weaving Shop** (Box 425, tel. 505/689–2437).

En Route   Continuing toward Taos, you'll come to the marvelous **San Tomás Church** in the village of Trampas, 7 mi north of Truchas on NM 76. It dates from at least 1760. To reach Rancho de Taos, the site of **San Francisco de Asís Church** (☞ Ranchos de Taos and Points South *in* Taos), continue north on NM 76 to its intersection with NM 75 and turn right (east). After 6 mi you'll come to NM 518. Make a left and drive 14 mi; the driveway leading to the church is 500 yards south of NM 518 on NM 68. Taos Plaza is about 4 mi north of the San Francisco de Asís on NM 68.

PUEBLOS NEAR SANTA FE

This trip will take you to several of the state's 19 pueblos, including San Ildefonso, one of the state's most picturesque, and Santa Clara, whose lands harbor a dramatic set of ancient cliff dwellings. Between the two reservations sits the ominous landmark called Black Mesa, which you can see from NM 30 or NM 502. The solitary butte has inspired many painters, including Georgia O'Keeffe. Plan on spending anywhere from one to three hours at each pueblo, and leave the day open if you are there for a feast day, when dances are set to an organic rather than mechanical clock. Pueblo grounds and hiking areas do not permit pets.

Pojoaque Pueblo

12 mi north of Santa Fe on U.S. 84/285.

There is not much to see in the pueblo's plaza area, which hardly has a visible core, but the state visitor center and adjoining **Poeh Cultural Center and Museum** on U.S. 84/285 are worth a visit. The latter is an impressive complex of traditional adobe buildings, including the three-story Sun Tower, which contains a museum, a cultural center, and artists' studios. There are frequent demonstrations by artists, exhibitions, and, in warm weather, traditional ceremonial dances. By the early 20th century the pueblo was virtually uninhabited, but the survivors eventually began to restore it. Pojoaque's feast day is celebrated with dancing on December 12. The visitor center is one of the friendliest and best stocked in northern New Mexico, with free maps and literature on hiking, fishing, and the area's history. Crafts in the visitor center are made by residents of Pojoaque and neighboring pueblos. *41 Camino de Rincon (Box 71), on U.S 84/285, Santa Fe 87501, tel. 505/455-3334. Free. Daily 8–5. Sketching, cameras, and video cameras are prohibited.*

Nambé Pueblo

Head north from Santa Fe past Tesuque on U.S. 84/285; about 12 mi out of town at Pojoaque turn northeast (right) onto NM 503. Nambé Pueblo is off NM 503 about 4 mi down a side road.

Nambé Pueblo no longer has a visitor center, so the best time to visit is during a ceremonial feast-day celebration on October 4, the feast day of St. Francis. If you want to explore the landscape surrounding the pueblo, take the drive past the pueblo until you come to Nambé Falls. There's a shady picnic area and a large fishing lake that's open from March to November. The waterfalls are about a 15-minute hike in from the parking and picnic area along a rocky, clearly marked path. The water pours over a rock precipice—a loud and dramatic sight given the modest size of the river. *Nambé Pueblo Rd. off NM 503, tel. 505/455–2036. $2.*

San Ildefonso Pueblo

19 mi north of Santa Fe on U.S. 84/285. From the Pojoaque Pueblo, return to U.S. 84/285, but exit almost immediately onto NM 502 toward Los Alamos. Continue for about 7 mi until you reach the turnoff for San Ildefonso.

Maria Martinez, one of the most renowned Pueblo potters, lived here. She first created her exquisite "black on black" pottery in 1919 and in doing so sparked a major revival of all Pueblo arts and crafts. She died in 1980, and the 26,000-acre San Ildefonso Pueblo remains a major center for pottery and other arts and crafts. Many artists sell from their homes, and there are trading posts, a visitor center, and a museum where some of Martinez's work can be seen on weekdays. San Ildefonso is also one of the more visually appealing pueblos, with a well-defined plaza core and a spectacular setting beneath the Pajarito Plateau and Black Mesa. The pueblo's feast day is January 23, when unforgettable buffalo, deer, and Comanche dances are performed from dawn to dusk. Cameras are not permitted at any of the ceremonial dances but may be used at other times with a permit.

On the western edge of the reservation is **Babbitt's Cottonwood Trading Post**, where John Babbitt continues the multigenerational tradition as a trader. Babbitt provides materials for making ceremonial costumes used during feast days. Ribbons, yarn and cloth, gourds for making rattles, and dried animal skins are among the goods he sells at this contemporary trading post. He also carries an excellent selection of 19th-century and new Navajo weavings. His expertise as a trader shows in the fine selection of Native American crafts for sale. NM 502, tel. 505/455–3549. $3 per car; still-camera permit $10, video recorder permit $20, sketching permit $15. Daily 8–5.

Santa Clara Pueblo

27 mi northwest of Santa Fe. From San Ildefonso Pueblo, return to NM 502 and continue west across the Rio Grande to NM 30. Turn north (right) and continue 6 mi to the turnoff to the Puyé Cliff Dwellings. Proceed on this gravel road 9 mi to Santa Clara Pueblo.

Santa Clara Pueblo, southwest of Española, is the home of an historic treasure—the awesome **Puyé Cliff Dwellings,** believed to have been built in the 13th and 14th centuries. They can be seen by driving 9 mi up a gravel road through a canyon, south of the village off NM 502. The pueblo also contains four ponds, miles of stream fishing, and picnicking and camping facilities. You can tour the cliff dwellings, topped by the ruins of a 740-room pueblo, on your own or with a guide. Permits for the use of trails, camping, and picnic areas, as well as for fishing in trout ponds, are available at the sites.

Shops in the village sell burnished red pottery, engraved blackware, paintings, and other arts and crafts. All pottery is made via the coil method, not with a pottery wheel. Santa Clara is known for its carved pieces, and Avanyu, a water serpent that guards the waters, is the pueblo's symbol. Other typical works include engagement baskets, wedding vessels, and seed pots. The pueblo's feast day of St. Clare is celebrated on August 12. Off NM 502 on NM 30, Española, tel. 505/753–7326. Pueblo free, cliff dwellings $5, video and still-camera permits $15. Daily 8–4:30.

OJO CALIENTE

55 mi north of Santa Fe on U.S. 285.

Ojo Caliente is the only place in North America where five different types of hot springs—iron, lithia, arsenic, salt, and soda—are found side by side. The town was named by Spanish explorer Cabeza de Vaca, who visited in 1535 and believed he had stumbled upon the Fountain of Youth. He recorded his excitement in his journal:

"The greatest treasure I have found these strange people to possess are some hot springs which burst out of the foot of a mountain that gives evidence of being an active volcano. So powerful are the chemicals contained in this water that the inhabitants have a belief that the waters were given to them by their gods after weeping many tears. From the effect of the waters upon my remaining men, I am inclined to believe that the waters will do many things that our doctors are not capable of doing . . . I believe I have found the Fountain of Youth."

Modern-day visitors draw similar conclusions about the restorative powers of the springs. The spa itself, built in the 1920s (no one knows the exact date), is a no-frills establishment that includes a hotel and cottages, a restaurant, a gift shop, massage rooms, men's and women's bathhouses, a chlorine-free swimming pool, and indoor and outdoor mineral-water tubs. The hotel, one of the original bathhouses, and the springs are all on the National Register of Historic Places, as is the adjacent Round Barn, from which visitors can take horseback tours and guided hikes to ancient pueblo dwellings and petroglyph-etched rocks. Spa services include wraps, massage, facials, and acupuncture. The setting at the foot of sandstone cliffs topped by the ruins of ancient Indian pueblos is nothing short of inspiring.

Smart Sightseeings

Savvy travelers and others who take their sightseeing seriously have skills worth knowing about.

DON'T PLAN YOUR VISIT IN YOUR HOTEL ROOM Don't wait until you pull into town to decide how to spend your days. It's inevitable that there will be much more to see and do than you'll have time for: choose sights in advance.

ORGANIZE YOUR TOURING Note the places that most interest you on a map, and visit places that are near each other during the same morning or afternoon.

START THE DAY WELL EQUIPPED Leave your hotel in the morning with everything you need for the day—maps, medicines, extra film, your guidebook, rain gear, and another layer of clothing in case the weather turns cooler.

TOUR MUSEUMS EARLY If you're there when the doors open you'll have an intimate experience of the collection.

EASY DOES IT See museums in the mornings, when you're fresh, and visit sit-down attractions later on. Take breaks before you need them.

STRIKE UP A CONVERSATION Only curmudgeons don't respond to a smile and a polite request for information. Most people appreciate your interest in their home town. And your conversations may end up being your most vivid memories.

GET LOST When you do, you never know what you'll find—but you can count on it being memorable. Use your guidebook to help you get back on track. Build wandering-around time into every day.

QUIT BEFORE YOU'RE TIRED There's no point in seeing that one extra sight if you're too exhausted to enjoy it.

TAKE YOUR MOTHER'S ADVICE Go to the bathroom when you have the chance. You never know what lies ahead.

Where to Stay

$$$ **OJO CALIENTE MINERAL SPRINGS SPA AND RESORT.**
Accommodations at this spa are decidedly spartan but clean and comfortable, with down comforters on the beds and rudimentary bathrooms without showers or tubs—you've come for the mineral springs, after all. Lodgers have complimentary access to the mineral pools and *milagro* (miracle) wraps, and the bathhouse is equipped with showers. The lodgings have no phones, but the morning newspaper is supplied. Some of the cottages have kitchenettes. Horseback tours of the area must be prearranged, so notify the office in advance. Poppy's Cafe serves New Mexican specialties for breakfast, lunch, and dinner. *50 Los Banos Dr., off U.S. 285, 30 mi north of Española (Box 68), 87549, tel. 505/583–2233 or 800/222–9162, fax 505/583–2464. 19 rooms, 19 cottages. Café.* AE, D, DC, MC, V. *www.ojocalientespa.com*

In This Chapter

Updated by Jeanie Puleston Fleming

taos

TAOS CASTS A LINGERING SPELL. The scent of piñon trees fills the air, and the fragrance of sagebrush is curiously strong here. Stately elms and cottonwoods frame sometimes narrow streets, and one- and two-story adobe buildings line the two-centuries-old Plaza. The adobes reveal the influence of Native American and Spanish settlers, and the entrepreneurial spirit here was brought by American traders. When it rains, the unpaved roads and lanes around town are not unlike the rutted streets of yesteryear.

With a population of about 6,500, Taos, on a rolling mesa at the base of the Sangre de Cristo Mountains, is actually three towns in one. The first is the low-key business district of art galleries, restaurants, and shops that recalls the Santa Fe of a few decades ago. The second area, 3 mi north of the commercial center, is Taos Pueblo, home to Tiwa-speaking Native Americans and also a UNESCO World Heritage site. Life at the Taos Pueblo long predates the arrival of the Spanish in America in the 1500s. Unlike many nomadic Native American tribes that were forced to relocate to government-designated reservations, the residents of Taos Pueblo have inhabited their land (at present 95,000 acres) at the base of the 12,282-ft-high Taos Mountain for centuries.

The third part of Taos, 4 mi south of town, is Ranchos de Taos, a farming and ranching community settled by the Spanish. Ranchos de Taos is best known for the San Francisco de Asís Church, whose buttressed adobe walls shelter significant religious artifacts and paintings. Its massive exterior and *camposanto* (graveyard) are among the most photographed in the country.

That so many 20th-century painters, photographers, and literary figures—among them Georgia O'Keeffe, Ansel Adams, and D. H. Lawrence—have been drawn to the earthy spirit of Taos has only heightened its appeal. Bert Geer Phillips and Ernest Leonard Blumenschein, traveling from Denver on a planned painting trip into Mexico in 1898, stopped in Taos to have a broken wagon wheel repaired. Enthralled with the landscape, earth-hue adobe buildings, piercing light, and clean mountain air, they abandoned their plan to journey farther south. They returned to the Taos area often, speaking so highly of it that other East Coast artists followed them west. By 1915, the Taos Society of Artists had been established. Blumenschein and Phillips, with Joseph Henry Sharp and Eanger Irving Couse, all graduates of the Paris art school Académie Julian, formed the core of the group.

Some of the early Taos artists spent their winters in New York or Chicago teaching painting or illustration to earn enough money to summer in New Mexico. Others became full-time New Mexicans. Living conditions were primitive then: no running water, electricity, or even indoor plumbing. But these painters happily endured such inconveniences to indulge their fascination with Native American customs, modes of dress, and ceremonies. Eventually, they co-opted the Native architecture and dress and presumptuously fancied that they "knew" Indian culture. The society disbanded in 1927, but Taos continued to attract artists. Several galleries opened and, in 1952, local painters joined together to form the Taos Artists' Association, forerunner to today's Taos Art Association. At present, several dozen galleries and shops display art, sculpture, and crafts, and about 1,000 artists live in town or nearby. No mere satellite of Santa Fe, Taos is an art center in its own right.

HERE AND THERE

Taos is small and resolutely rustic, and the central area is highly walkable. Sociable Taoseños make the town an even more welcoming place to explore. You'll need a car to reach the Enchanted Circle, the Rio Grande Gorge, Taos Ski Valley, and other places of interest beyond Taos proper. Traffic can be heavy in the peak summer and winter seasons; ask locals about back roads that let you avoid backed-up ones like Paseo del Pueblo.

The Museum Association of Taos includes seven properties. Among them are the Harwood Museum, the Fechin Institute, the Millicent Rogers Museum, and the Van Vechten–Lineberry Taos Art Museum, as well as those in the Kit Carson Historic Museum consortium: the Blumenschein Home and Museum, the Kit Carson Home and Museum, and La Hacienda de los Martínez. Each of the museums charges $4 or $5 for admission, but you can opt for a combination ticket—30% discount on all seven valid for one year, or buy a $10 joint ticket to the three Kit Carson museums.

DOWNTOWN TAOS

More than four centuries after it was laid out, Taos Plaza remains the center of commercial life in Taos. Bent Street, where New Mexico's first American governor lived and died, is the town's upscale shopping area and gallery enclave.

Numbers in the margin correspond to numbers on the Exploring Taos map.

Sights to See

❷ BLUMENSCHEIN HOME AND MUSEUM. For an introduction to the history of the Taos art scene, start with Ernest L. Blumenschein's residence, which provides a glimpse into the cosmopolitan lives led by the members of the Taos Society of Artists, of which Blumenschein was a founding member. One of the rooms in the

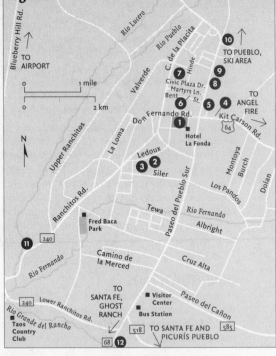

Blumenschein Home and Museum, 2

Fechin Institute, 9

Firehouse Collection, 7

Governor Bent Museum, 6

Harwood Foundation, 3

Kit Carson Home and Museum, 4

Kit Carson Memorial Park, 8

La Hacienda de los Martínez, 11

San Francisco de Asís Church, 12

Stables Art Center, 5

Taos Plaza, 1

Van Vechten – Lineberry Taos Art Museum, 10

adobe-style structure dates from 1797. On display are the art, antiques, and other personal possessions of Blumenschein and his wife, Mary Greene Blumenschein, who also painted, as did their daughter Helen. Several of Ernest Blumenschein's vivid oil paintings hang in his former studio, and also on display are works by other early Taos artists. *222 Ledoux St., tel. 505/758–0505. $5 (or use Kit Carson Historic Museums of Taos joint ticket). Apr.–Oct., daily 9–5; Nov.–Mar., daily 11–4.*

★ **❾ FECHIN INSTITUTE.** The interior of this extraordinary adobe house, built between 1927 and 1933 by Russian émigré and artist Nicolai Fechin, is a marvel of carved Russian-style woodwork and furniture that glisten with an almost golden sheen. Fechin constructed it to showcase his daringly colorful portraits and landscapes. Fechin's octogenarian daughter Eya oversees her father's architectural masterpiece—she loves talking about him and life "back then." Listed on the National Register of Historic Places, the Fechin Institute hosts exhibits and special workshops devoted to the artist's unique approach to learning, teaching, and creating. Open hours are often in flux, so call ahead. *227 Paseo del Pueblo Norte, tel. 505/758–1710. $3. Wed.–Sun. 10–2.*

🌀 **❼ FIREHOUSE COLLECTION.** More than 100 works by well-known Taos artists like Joseph Sharp, Ernest L. Blumenschein, and Bert Phillips hang in the Taos Volunteer Fire Department building. The exhibition space adjoins the station house, where five fire engines are maintained at the ready and an antique fire engine is on display. *323 Camino de la Placita, tel. 505/758–3386. Free. Weekdays 8–4:30.*

🌀 **❻ GOVERNOR BENT MUSEUM.** In 1846, when New Mexico became a U.S. possession as a result of the Mexican War, Charles Bent, a trader, trapper, and mountain man, was appointed governor. Less than a year later he was killed in his house by an angry mob protesting New Mexico's annexation by the United States. Governor Bent was married to María Ignacia, the older sister of

Josefa Jaramillo, the wife of mountain man Kit Carson. A collection of Native American artifacts, Western Americana, and family possessions is squeezed into five small rooms of the adobe building where Bent and his family lived. 117A Bent St., tel. 505/758–2376. $1. Daily 10–5.

★ **3 HARWOOD FOUNDATION.** The Pueblo Revival former home of Burritt Elihu "Burt" Harwood, a dedicated painter who studied in France before moving to Taos with his public-spirited wife, Lucy, in 1916, is adjacent to a museum dedicated to the works of local artists. Traditional Hispanic northern New Mexican artists, early art-colony painters, post–World War II modernists, and contemporary artists such as Larry Bell, Agnes Martin, Ken Price, and Earl Stroh are represented. Mabel Dodge Luhan, a major arts patron, bequeathed many of the 19th-century and early 20th-century works in the Harwoods' collection, including *retablos* (painted wood representations of Catholic saints) and *bultos* (three-dimensional carvings of the saints). In the Hispanic Traditions Gallery upstairs are 19th-century tinwork, furniture, and sculpture. Downstairs, among early 20th-century art-colony holdings, look for E. Martin Hennings's *Chamisa in Bloom*, featuring the familiar New Mexican gray-green plant tipped with golden fall flowers and backed by a blue ridge of mountains. A tour of the ground-floor galleries shows that Taos painters of the era, notably Oscar Berninghaus, Ernest Blumenschein, Victor Higgins, Walter Ufer, Marsden Hartley, and John Marin, were fascinated by the land and the people linked to it. An octagonal gallery exhibits works by Agnes Martin. Martin's seven large canvas panels (5 ft by 5 ft) are studies in white paint, their precise lines and blocks forming textured grids. Operated by the University of New Mexico since 1936, the Harwood is the second oldest art museum in the state. 238 Ledoux St., tel. 505/758–9826. $5. Tues.–Sat. 10–5, Sun. noon–5.

🖐 **4 KIT CARSON HOME AND MUSEUM.** Kit Carson bought this low-slung 12-room adobe home in 1843 as a wedding gift for Josefa

Jaramillo, the daughter of a powerful, politically influential Spanish family. Josefa was 14 when the dashing, twice-married mountain man and scout began courting her. Three of the museum's rooms are furnished as they were when the Carson family lived here. The rest of the museum is devoted to gun and mountain-man exhibits, such as rugged leather clothing and Kit's own Spencer carbine rifle with its beaded leather carrying case, and early Taos antiques, artifacts, and manuscripts. *Kit Carson Rd., tel. 505/758–4741. $5 (or use Kit Carson Historic Museums of Taos joint ticket). Nov. 2–Apr., daily 9–5; May–Nov. 1, daily 8–6.*

NEED A BREAK? **Caffe Tazza** (122 Kit Carson Rd., tel. 505/758–8706) serves great coffee, chai tea, and Italian sodas as well as pastries and vegetarian chili inside by the photo display or on the outside terrace. Or, let the coffee aroma draw you into the tiny **World Cup** (102 Paseo del Pueblo Norte, tel. 505/737–5299).

8 KIT CARSON MEMORIAL PARK. The noted pioneer is buried in the park that bears his name. His grave is marked with a *cerquita* (a spiked wrought-iron rectangular fence), traditionally used to outline and protect burial sites. Also interred here is Mabel Dodge Luhan, the pioneering patron of the early Taos art scene. The 20-acre park has swings and slides for recreational breaks. It's well marked with big stone pillars and a gate. *Paseo del Pueblo Norte at Civic Plaza Dr., tel. 505/758–8234. Free. Memorial Day–Labor Day, daily 8–8; Labor Day–Memorial Day, daily 8–5.*

5 STABLES ART CENTER. It was in the stables in back of this house that the Taos Artists' Association first began showing the works of members and invited nonmember artists from across northern New Mexico. In 1952 the association purchased the handsome adobe building, which is now the visual arts gallery of the Taos Art Association. All the work on exhibit is for sale. *133 Paseo del Pueblo Norte, tel. 505/758–2036. Free. Daily 10–5.*

❶ TAOS PLAZA. The first European explorers of the Taos Valley came here with Captain Hernando de Alvarado, a member of Francisco Vásquez de Coronado's expedition of 1540. Basque explorer Don Juan de Oñate arrived in Taos in July 1598 and established a mission and trading arrangements with residents of Taos Pueblo. The settlement actually developed into two plazas: the Plaza at the heart of the town became a thriving business district for the early colony; a walled residential plaza was constructed a few hundred yards behind; it remains active today, home to a throng of gift and coffee shops. As authorized by a special act of Congress, the American flag flies in the center of the Plaza day and night in recognition of Kit Carson's heroic stand protecting it from Confederate sympathizers during the Civil War. The covered gazebo was donated by heiress and longtime Taos resident Mabel Dodge Luhan. On the southeastern corner of Taos Plaza is the **Hotel La Fonda de Taos**. Some infamous erotic paintings by D. H. Lawrence that were naughty in his day but are quite tame by present standards can be viewed ($2 entry fee) in the former barroom beyond the lobby. As an accommodation, the hotel is in need of renovations.

NEED A BREAK? To fuel your walk, grab a pick-me-up at the **Bent Street Coffeehouse** (124-F Bent St., tel. 505/751–7184).

❿ VAN VECHTEN–LINEBERRY TAOS ART MUSEUM. This privately run museum shows the works of painter Duane Van Vechten, the late wife of Edwin C. Lineberry. Her former studio is the entrance to the museum, whose collection of about 130 works by more than 50 Taos artists includes works of varying quality by all of the founders of the Taos Society of Artists. The museum's signature piece is *Our Lady of Gualadupe* (1929) by Van Vechten, a painting of a solid adobe church against a deep blue sky. On a par with the exhibits are the museum grounds, a 10-acre, walled park, and the building itself, which was the home of the artist and Mr.

Lineberry, who maintains the museum with his wife, Novella. 501 *Paseo del Norte, tel. 505/758–2690. $6. Wed.–Fri. 11–4, weekends 1:30–4.*

RANCHOS DE TAOS AND POINTS SOUTH

The first Spanish settlers were farmers who faced raids by non–Pueblo Indians like the Comanches. Aspects of this history come alive on this meandering drive south through fields and farmland to a restored hacienda and into a former farming village with its famous, fortresslike church.

Numbers in the margin correspond to numbers on the Exploring Taos map.

Sights to See

⓫ **LA HACIENDA DE LOS MARTÍNEZ.** Spare and fortlike, this adobe structure built between 1804 and 1827 on the bank of the Rio Pueblo served as a community refuge during Comanche and Apache raids. Its thick walls, which have few windows, surround two central courtyards. Don Antonio Severino Martínez was a farmer and trader; the hacienda was the final stop along El Camino Real (the Royal Road), the trade route the Spanish established between Mexico City and New Mexico. The restored period rooms here contain textiles, foods, and crafts of the early 19th century. There's a working blacksmith's shop, and weavers create beautiful textiles on reconstructed period looms. During the last weekend in September the hacienda hosts the Old Taos Trade Fair, a reenactment of fall trading fairs of the 1820s, when Plains Indians and trappers came to Taos to trade with the Spanish and the Pueblo Indians. The two-day event includes crafts demonstrations, native foods, and entertainment. *Ranchitos Rd. (NM 240), tel. 505/758–1000. $5 (or use Kit Carson Historic Museums of Taos joint ticket). Apr.–Oct., daily 9–5; Nov.–Mar., daily 10–4.*

OFF THE **PICURÍS PUEBLO** – The Picurís (Keresan for "those who paint")
BEATEN Native Americans once lived in six- and seven-story dwellings
PATH similar to those still standing at the Taos Pueblo, but these were

abandoned in the wake of 18th-century Pueblo uprisings. Relatively isolated about 30 mi south of Taos, Picurís, one of the smallest pueblos in New Mexico, is surrounded by the timberland of the Carson National Forest. The 270-member Tiwa-speaking Picurís tribe is a sovereign nation and has no treaties with any country, including the United States. You can tour the village and 700-year-old ruins of kivas (ceremonial rooms) and storage areas, which were excavated in 1961. The exhibits in the pueblo's museum include pottery and some ruins. A separate building under renovation will contain a restaurant. The uncompleted convenience store and crafts shop are occasionally open. Fishing, picnicking, and camping are allowed at nearby trout-stocked Pu-Na and Tu-Tah lakes. Fishing and camping permits can be obtained at the Picurís Market. The pueblo honors its patron saint, San Lorenzo, with a festival on August 9 and 10. *NM 75, Peñasco (from Ranchos de Taos head south on NM 518, east on NM 75, and turn right at signs for village; from NM 68 head east on NM 75 and make a left into village), tel. 505/587–2519. Museum free, self-guided walking or driving tours $1.75, still camera permit $5 (includes $1.75 fee for camera-holder), video camera or sketching permit $10 (includes $1.75 fee). Daily 9–6, but call ahead especially Labor Day–Memorial Day, when the pueblo is sometimes closed.*

RANCHOS DE TAOS. A few minutes' drive south of the center of Taos, this village still retains some of its rural atmosphere despite the highway traffic passing through. Huddled around its famous adobe church and dusty plaza are cheerful, remodeled shops and galleries standing shoulder to shoulder with crumbling adobe shells. This ranching, farming, and budding small-business community was an early home to Taos Native Americans before being settled by Spaniards in 1716. Although many of the adobe dwellings have seen better days, the shops, modest galleries, taco stands, and two fine restaurants point to an ongoing revival. The massive bulk of **San Francisco de Asís**

Church (☞ *below*) is an enduring attraction. *Paseo del Pueblo Sur (NM 68), about 4 mi south of Taos Plaza.*

⑫ SAN FRANCISCO DE ASÍS CHURCH. The Spanish Mission–style church was erected in the 18th century as a spiritual and physical refuge from raiding Apaches, Utes, and Comanches. In 1979 the deteriorated church was rebuilt with traditional adobe bricks by community volunteers. Every spring a group gathers to re-mud the facade. The earthy, clean lines of the exterior walls and supporting bulwarks have inspired generations of painters and photographers. The late-afternoon light provides the best exposure of the heavily buttressed rear of the church—though today's image-takers face the challenge of framing the architecturally pure lines through rows of parked cars and a large, white sign put up by church officials; morning light is best for the front. Bells in the twin belfries call Taoseños to services on Sunday and holidays. In the parish hall nearby a 15-minute video presentation every half hour describes the history and restoration of the church and explains the mysterious painting, *Shadow of the Cross,* on which each evening the shadow of a cross appears over Christ's shoulder. Scientific studies made on the canvas and the paint pigments cannot explain the phenomenon. *NM 68, 500 yards south of NM 518, Ranchos de Taos, tel. 505/758–2754. $2. Mon.–Sat. 9–4, Sun. and holy days during morning church services: Mass at 7 (in Spanish), 9, and 11:30.*

NEED A
BREAK?
The storefront **Ranchos Coffee Company** (1807 Paseo del Pueblo Sur, tel. 505/751–0653) has fresh coffee, tea, pastries, and sandwiches.

TAOS PUEBLO TO RIO GRANDE GORGE

Numbers in the margin correspond to numbers on the Taos Pueblo and the Enchanted Circle map.

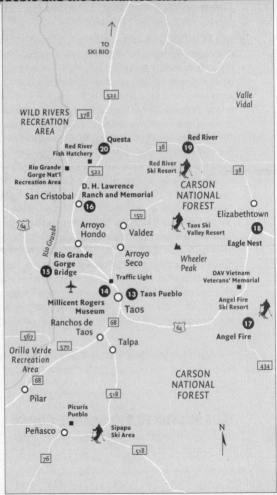

TO
SKI RIO

Valle
Vidal

522

WILD RIVERS
RECREATION
AREA

378

Red River
Fish Hatchery

Questa

20

38

Red River

19

Red River
Ski Resort

38

Rio Grande
Gorge Nat'l
Recreation Area

522

D. H. Lawrence
Ranch and Memorial

San Cristobal

16

CARSON
NATIONAL
FOREST

Elizabethtown

Arroyo
Hondo

150

Valdez

Taos Ski
Valley Resort

18

Rio Grande

Arroyo
Seco

Eagle Nest

Rio Grande
Gorge
Bridge

15

Wheeler
Peak

64

Traffic Light

DAV Vietnam
Veterans' Memorial

14

13

Taos Pueblo

Millicent Rogers
Museum

Taos

Angel Fire
Ski Resort

Ranchos de
Taos

68

64

17

567

Talpa

Angel Fire

Orilla Verde
Recreation
Area

570

434

68

CARSON
NATIONAL
FOREST

Pilar

518

Picurís
Pueblo

N

Peñasco

Sipapu
Ski Area

76

518

Sights to See

⑭ MILLICENT ROGERS MUSEU~~M~~
American and Hispanic art,
Millicent Rogers's private colle~~ction~~
blankets, rugs, jewelry, katsina ~~d~~
religious and secular artifacts
pottery and ceramics of Maria ~~Martinez~~
San Ildefonso Pueblo. Docen~~t~~
appointment, and the museum h~~osts~~ ~~wor~~kshops,
and demonstrations. 1504 Museum ~~(from~~ Taos Plaza head north
on Paseo del Pueblo Norte and left at the sign for County Rd. BA030—
also called Millicent Rogers Rd. or Museum Rd.), tel. 505/758–2462.
$6. Apr.–Sept., daily 10–5; Nov.–Mar., Tues.–Sun. 10–5.

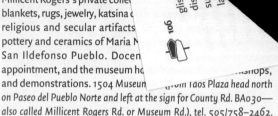

🖐 ⑮ RIO GRANDE GORGE BRIDGE. It's a breathtaking experience to
see the Rio Grande flowing 650 ft underfoot. The bridge is the
second-highest expansion bridge in the country. Hold on to your
camera and eyeglasses when looking down, and watch out for
low-flying planes. The Taos Municipal Airport is close by, and
daredevil private pilots have been known to challenge one another
to fly under the bridge. Shortly after daybreak, hot air balloons
fly above and even inside the gorge.

★ 🖐 ⑬ TAOS PUEBLO. For nearly 1,000 years the mud-and-straw adobe
walls of Taos Pueblo have sheltered Tiwa-speaking Native
Americans. A United Nations World Heritage Site, this is the
largest multistory pueblo structure in the United States. The two
main buildings, Hlauuma (north house) and Hlaukwima (south
house), separated by a creek, are believed to be of a similar age,
probably constructed between 1000 and 1450. The dwellings
have common walls but no connecting doorways—the Tiwas
gained access only from the top, via ladders that were retrieved
after entering. Small buildings and corrals are scattered about.

The pueblo today appears much as it did when the first Spanish
explorers arrived in New Mexico in 1540. The adobe walls

mica caused the conquistadors to believe they had [...] one of the fabled Seven Cities of Gold. The outside [...] are continuously maintained by replastering with thin [...] of mud, and the interior walls are frequently coated with thin washes of white clay. Some walls are several feet thick in places. The roofs of each of the five-story structures are supported by large timbers, or vigas, hauled down from the mountain forests. Pine or aspen *latillas* (smaller pieces of wood) are placed side by side between the vigas; the entire roof is then packed with dirt.

Even after 400 years of Spanish and Anglo presence in Taos, inside the pueblo the traditional Native American way of life has endured. Tribal custom allows no electricity or running water in Hlauuma and Hlaukwima, where varying numbers (usually fewer than 100) of Taos Native Americans live full-time. About 2,000 others live in conventional homes on the pueblo's 95,000 acres. The crystal-clear Rio Pueblo de Taos, originating high above in the mountains at the sacred Blue Lake, is the primary source of water for drinking and irrigating. Bread is still baked in *hornos* (outdoor domed ovens). Artisans of the Taos Pueblo produce and sell (tax-free) traditionally handcrafted wares such as mica-flecked pottery and silver jewelry. Great hunters, the Taos Native Americans are also known for their work with animal skins and their excellent moccasins, boots, and drums.

Although the population is about 90% Catholic, the people of Taos Pueblo, like most Pueblo Native Americans, also maintain their native religious traditions. At Christmas and other sacred holidays, for instance, immediately after Mass, dancers dressed in seasonal sacred garb proceed down the aisle of St. Jerome Chapel, drums beating and rattles shaking, to begin other religious rites.

The pueblo **Church of San Geronimo**, or St. Jerome, the patron saint of Taos Pueblo, was completed in 1850 to replace the one destroyed by the U.S. Army in 1847 during the Mexican War. With its smooth symmetry, stepped portal, and twin bell towers, the church is a popular subject for photographers and artists (though the taking of photographs inside is discouraged).

The public is invited to certain ceremonial dances held throughout the year: January 1, Turtle Dance; January 6, Buffalo or Deer Dance; May 3, Feast of Santa Cruz Foot Race and Corn Dance; June 13, Feast of San Antonio Corn Dance; June 24, Feast of San Juan Corn Dance; July 2 weekend, Taos Pueblo Powwow; July 25–26, Feast of Santa Ana and Santiago Corn Dance; September 29–30, Feast of San Geronimo Sunset Dance; Christmas Eve, the Procession; Christmas Day, Deer Dance or Matachines. While you're at the pueblo certain rules must be observed: respect the RESTRICTED AREA signs that protect the privacy of residents and native religious sites; do not enter private homes or open any doors not clearly labeled as curio shops; do not photograph tribal members without asking permission; do not enter the cemetery grounds; and do not wade in the Rio Pueblo de Taos, which is considered sacred and is the community's sole source of drinking water. *Head to the right off Paseo del Pueblo Norte just past the Best Western Kachina Lodge, tel. 505/758–1028. Tourist fees $10. Guided tours by appointment. Still-camera permit $10 (note: cameras that may look commercial such as those with telephoto lenses, might be denied a permit); video-camera permit $20; commercial photography, sketching, or painting only by prior permission from the governor's office (505/ 758–1028); fees vary; apply at least 10 days in advance. Apr.–Nov., daily 8–4; Oct.–Mar., daily 8:30–4. Closed for funerals, religious ceremonies, and for a 2-month "quiet time" in late winter or early spring, and the last part of Aug.; call ahead before visiting at these times.*

NEED A BREAK? Look for signs that read FRY BREAD on dwellings in the pueblo: you can enter the kitchen and buy a piece of fresh bread dough that is flattened and deep-fried until puffy and golden brown and then topped with honey or powdered sugar.

THE ENCHANTED CIRCLE

Some clever marketers conceived the moniker the Enchanted Circle to describe the territory accessed by the roads that form an 84-mi loop north from Taos and back to town (U.S. 64 to NM 522 to NM 38 back to U.S. 64), and it's likely you'll agree with their choice. A trip around the Enchanted Circle includes a glorious panorama of alpine valleys and the towering mountains of the lush Carson National Forest. You can see all the major sights listed below on a one-day drive.

Numbers in the margin correspond to numbers on the Taos Pueblo and the Enchanted Circle map.

Sights To See

⑲ ANGEL FIRE. For hundreds of years a long, empty valley and the fall meeting grounds of the Ute Indians, the Angel Fire area is a busy ski resort these days. There are several dining options at the main resort. A prominent landmark is the **DAV Vietnam Veterans Memorial,** a 50-ft-high wing-shaped monument built in 1971 by D. Victor Westphall, whose son David was killed in Vietnam. The memorial's textured surface, which captures the dazzling, colorful reflections of the New Mexican mountains, changes constantly with the sun's movement. *U.S. 64, 25 mi east of Taos, tel. 505/377–6401 (24 hrs) or 800/633–7463 (8–5).*

CARSON NATIONAL FOREST. The national forest that surrounds Taos spans almost 200 mi across northern New Mexico and encompasses mountains, lakes, streams, villages, and much of the Enchanted Circle. Hiking, skiing, horseback riding, mountain biking, backpacking, trout fishing, boating, and wildflower viewing are among the popular activities here. The forest is home to big-game animals and many species of smaller animals and songbirds. **Wheeler Peak** is a designated wilderness area where travel is restricted to hiking or horseback riding. Contact the Carson National Forest for maps, safety guidelines, and conditions (it's open weekdays 8–4:30). *Forest Service Building, 208 Cruz Alta Rd., Taos 87571, tel. 505/758–6200.*

16 D. H. LAWRENCE RANCH AND MEMORIAL. The influential and controversial English writer David Herbert Lawrence and his wife, Frieda, arrived in Taos at the invitation of Mabel Dodge Luhan, who collected famous writers and artists the way some people collect butterflies. Luhan provided them a place to live, Kiowa Ranch, on 160 acres in the mountains. Rustic and remote, it's known as the D. H. Lawrence Ranch, though Lawrence never actually owned it. Lawrence lived in Taos on and off for about 22 months during a three-year period between 1922 and 1925. He wrote his novel *The Plumed Serpent* (1926), as well as some of his finest short stories and poetry, while in Taos and on excursions to Mexico. The houses here, owned by the University of New Mexico, are not open to the public; the nearby smaller cabin is where Dorothy Brett, the Lawrences' traveling companion, stayed. You can visit the D. H. Lawrence Memorial on wooded Lobo Mountain. A white shedlike structure, it's simple and unimposing. The writer fell ill while visiting France and died in a sanatorium there in 1930. Five years later Frieda had Lawrence's body disinterred and cremated and brought his ashes back to Taos. Frieda Lawrence is buried, as was her wish, in front of the memorial. Views down into the Taos area to the south and west are great. *NM 522 (follow signed dirt road from the highway), San Cristobal, tel. 505/776–2245. Free. Daily dawn–dusk.*

20 EAGLE NEST. Eagle Nest Lake nestles into the crook made by the intersection of NM 64 and NM 38, and the main street through town is actually NM 64. Thousands of acres of national forest surround this funky village, population 189, elevation 8,090 ft. The shops and other buildings here evoke New Mexico's mining heritage while a 1950s-style diner, Kaw-Lija's, serves up a memorable burger. *NM 38, 14 mi north of Angel Fire.*

22 **QUESTA.** In the heart of the Sangre de Cristo Mountains, Questa, literally, "hill," is a quiet village about 12 mi from the town of Red River, nestled against the Red River itself and amid some of the most striking mountain country in New Mexico. **St. Anthony's Church,** built of adobe with 5-ft-thick walls and viga ceilings, is on the main street. Questa's **Cabresto Lake,** in Carson National Forest, is about 8 mi from town. Follow NM 563 to Forest Route 134, then 2 mi of a primitive road (134A)—you'll need a four-wheel-drive vehicle. You can trout fish and boat here from about June to October.

21 **RED RIVER.** A major ski resort, Red River, elevation 8,750 ft, came into being as a miners' boomtown during the 19th century, taking its name from the river whose mineral content gave it a rich, rosy color. When the gold petered out, Red River died, only to be rediscovered in the 1920s by migrants escaping the dust storms in the Great Plains. An Old West flavor remains: Main Street shoot-outs, an authentic melodrama, and square dancing and two-stepping are among the diversions here. Because of its many country dances and festivals, Red River is affectionately called "The New Mexico Home of the Texas Two-Step." The bustling little downtown area contains shops and sportswear boutiques. The **Jewelry Lady** (Main St., tel. 505/754–2300) is a well-stocked shop. The ski area is also in the middle of town, with lifts within walking distance of restaurants and hotels. *Off NM 38, tel. 505/ 776–5510 for overnight reservations.*

NEED A BREAK? In Red River stop by the **Sundance** (High St., tel. 505/754–2971) for Mexican food. **Texas Red's Steakhouse** (Main St., tel. 505/ 754–2964) has steaks, chops, burgers, and chicken. The **Black Crow Coffeehouse** (Main St., tel. 505/754–3150) serves up an energizing brew.

RED RIVER HATCHERY. At this engaging facility you can feed freshwater trout and learn how they're hatched, reared, stocked, and controlled. The visitor center has displays and exhibits, a show pond, and a machine that dispenses fish food. The self-guided tour can last anywhere from 20 to 90 minutes, depending on how enraptured you become. There's a picnic area on the grounds. *NM 522, 5 mi south of Questa, tel. 505/586–0222. Free. Daily 8–5.*

EATING OUT

For a place as remote as Taos, the dining scene is surprisingly varied and well supplied with foods from outside the area. You can find the usual coffee shops and Mexican-style eateries but also restaurants serving creatively prepared Continental, Italian, and Southwestern cuisine. Arroyo Seco, a village about 7 mi north of Taos on the way to Taos Ski Valley, has several good eateries. For price categories, *see* the chart *under Dining in* Practical Information.

DOWNTOWN TAOS
American

$$–$$$ **OGELVIE'S BAR AND GRILL.** On the second floor of an old two-story adobe building, Ogelvie's is the perfect spot for people-watching from on high, especially from the outdoor patio in summer. You won't find any culinary surprises here, just dependable meat-and-potato dishes. The sure bets are Angus beef, grilled Rocky Mountain trout, and meat or cheese enchiladas. *East side of Taos Plaza, tel. 505/758–8866. Reservations not accepted. AE, DC, MC, V.*

$–$$ **MICHAEL'S KITCHEN.** This casual, homey restaurant serves up a bit of everything—you can order a hamburger while your friend who can't get enough chile can order another enchilada. Brunch is popular with the locals, and amusing asides to the waitstaff over the intercom contribute to the energetic buzz. Breakfast, lunch, and dinner are served daily, but be sure to order dinner by 8:30.

taos dining

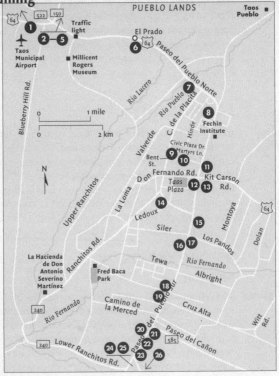

304 Paseo del Pueblo Norte, tel. 505/758–4 accepted. AE, D, MC, V.

$ **ESKE'S BREW PUB.** This casual dining an by off-duty ski patrollers and river guides hearty sandwiches with soup and salad. downstairs produces everything from nutty, dark stout There's live music on weekends. 106 Des Georges La., tel. 505/758–1517. MC, V.

Contemporary

$$$–$$$$ **DOC MARTIN'S.** The restaurant of the Taos Inn takes its name from the building's original owner, a local physician who performed operations and delivered babies in rooms that are now the dining areas. Among the signature creations are the piñon-crusted salmon and the Aztec chocolate mousse with roasted-banana sauce. The wine list has won awards from *Wine Spectator* and other organizations. Taos Inn, 125 Paseo del Pueblo Norte, tel. 505/758–1977. MC, V.

$$–$$$$ **LAMBERT'S OF TAOS.** The signature dishes at this restaurant 2½ blocks south of the Plaza include crab cakes and pepper-crusted lamb. California's finest vintages receive top billing on the wine list. The desserts are tasty. Randall House, 309 Paseo del Pueblo Sur, tel. 505/758–1009. AE, DC, MC, V. No lunch weekends.

$$–$$$ **APPLE TREE.** Named for the large tree in the umbrella-shaded courtyard, this is a great lunch and early dinner spot in a historic adobe a block from the Plaza. The food is fresh—among the well-crafted dishes are grilled lamb and chicken fajitas. The restaurant has received regular awards for its wine selection, which includes many options by the glass. Sunday brunch is served from 10 to 3. Expect about a 15-minute wait if you don't have a reservation. There's an aromatherapy shop upstairs and a coffee and juice bar outside. 123 Bent St., tel. 505/758–1900. AE, D, DC, MC, V.

$$–$$$ **BYZANTIUM.** Off a grassy courtyard near the Blumenschein and Harwood museums, this restaurant offers an eclectic menu with

ouches of Asia, the Middle East, and Europe in dishes such as Wu Tang chicken, baba ghanoush, grilled polenta, and green lip mussel hot pot. *Ledoux St. and La Placita, tel. 505/751–0805. AE, MC, V. Closed Tues. No lunch.*

$$ LA LUNA. In a colorful two-level space with a mural along one wall, the former New Yorkers who took charge in late 1999 have attracted a local clientele fond of the pasta such as the penne with cilantro-citrus sauce, the daily fish specials, and the pizza from the wood-fired oven in the dining room. Also for sale: bottles of the house apple-balsamic vinaigrette. *225 Paseo del Pueblo Sur, tel. 505/751–0023. AE, D, MC, V. No lunch Sun.*

$–$$ BRAVO! Short on atmosphere but by no means tacky, this restaurant and full bar inside an upscale grocery store and beer and wine shop is a great stop for gourmet picnic fixings or an on-site meal. The fare is nothing if not varied—you can feast on anything from a turkey sandwich to escargots—and there's a children's menu to boot. The beer and wine selection is formidable. *1353A Paseo del Pueblo Sur, tel. 505/758–8100. Reservations not accepted. MC, V. Closed Sun.*

Deli

$$–$$$ BENT STREET DELI. Great soups, sandwiches, salads, and desserts (cheesecake and other sweet treats) are the trademarks of the small and unassuming Bent Street Deli, which serves beer, wine, and gourmet coffees. Reubens are on the menu for East Coasters and others who can't live without a dose of pastrami. Dinners are a little fancier: fresh salmon, Sumatra primavera pasta with Indonesian peanut sauce, or shrimp in pesto sauce. Breakfast is served until 11 AM. *120 Bent St., tel. 505/758–5787. MC, V. Closed Sun.*

$ JJ'S BAGELS. In a storefront off the tourist path, this cybercafé bakes bagels on the spot and serves pastries, soups, and sandwiches along with Internet connections. Take out picnic fare or choose a table and terminal. It's open 7–5 weekdays and 7–2 weekends. 710 Paseo del Pueblo Sur, tel. 505/758–0045. MC, V.

$ TAOS WRAPPERS. Owner-chefs Kim Wever and Greg Payton have a loyal clientele for take-out lunch, and a small eat-in space with tiny tables. Pesto chicken, roasted veggies, and curried tuna are among the healthful ingredients inside flavored tortilla wraps. There are soups, salads, and desserts, too. 616 Paseo del Pueblo Sur, tel. 505/751–9727. No credit cards.

Southwestern

$$–$$$ CASA DE VALDEZ. A large A-frame building with wood-panel walls and beamed ceilings, Casa de Valdez has the feel of a mountain lodge. The tables and chairs are handmade, as are the colorful drapes on the windows. Owner-chef Peter Valdez specializes in hickory-smoked barbecues, charcoal-grilled steaks, and regional New Mexican cuisine. 1401 Paseo del Pueblo Sur, tel. 505/758–8777. AE, D, MC, V. Closed Wed.

$$–$$$ JACQUELINA'S. Specializing in fare of northern New Mexico, this ★ restaurant on the south end of town has a following among longtime Taos residents. The night's menu might include a grilled salmon with tomatillo salsa or barbecued shrimp with *poblano* (a dark green, rich-tasting chile, ranging from mild to fiery) corn salsa. 1541 Paseo del Pueblo Sur, tel. 505/751–0399. MC, V. Closed Mon. No lunch Sat.

$$ FRED'S PLACE. Eccentric decorations—carved crucifixes and santos and a ceiling mural of hell—set a quirky tone at this hip spot with a congenial staff. You may have to stand in line at popular Fred's, but you'll find you haven't waited in vain when you taste the subtly prepared northern New Mexican specialties like *carne adovada* (meat marinated in a spicy sauce) and blue-corn enchiladas. 332 Paseo del Pueblo Sur, tel. 505/758–0514. Reservations not accepted. MC, V. Closed Sun. No lunch.

$ GUADALAJARA GRILL. Tasty Mexican cuisine is the feature here, served quickly from the open, spotless kitchens and popular enough with local patrons that there is one on each end of town. You'll hear Spanish banter across the kitchen counter while you watch your burritos or enchiladas being prepared. *822 Paseo del Pueblo Norte, tel. 505/737–0816; 1384 Paseo del Pueblo Sur, tel. 505/ 751–0063. MC, V.*

$ ORLANDO'S. This family-run local favorite features authentic-tasting *carne adovada* (red chile–marinated pork), blue-corn enchiladas, and an innovative shrimp burrito, among other offerings. Eat in the cozy dining room or call ahead for takeout. *114 Don Juan Valdez La., off Paseo des Pueblo Norte, tel. 505/751–1450. No credit cards. Closed Sun.*

RANCHOS DE TAOS AND POINTS SOUTH
American

$$$–$$$$ STAKEOUT GRILL AND BAR. On Outlaw Hill in the foothills of the Sangre de Cristo Mountains, this old adobe homestead has 100-mi-long views and sunsets that dazzle. The sturdy fare includes New York strip steaks, filet mignon, pepper steak, shrimp scampi, swordfish steaks, duck, chicken, and daily pasta specials. The restaurant's decor will take you back to the days of the Wild West even though the owners hail from northern Italy. *Stakeout Dr., 8½ mi south of Taos Plaza, east of NM 68 (look for the huge cowboy hat), tel. 505/758–2042. AE, D, DC, MC, V.*

Contemporary

$$$–$$$$ JOSEPH'S TABLE. The funky decor and romantic lighting at Joseph's make a rustic yet dramatic stage for Italian-oriented fare like the gnocchi stuffed with white-truffle paste, seared salmon with tarragon velouté, and the pepper steak with garlic mashed red potatoes. The first-rate desserts are more ornate. *4167*

Paseo del Pueblo Sur (NM 68), Ranchos de Taos,
D, DC, MC, V. Closed Mon., Tues. No lunch.

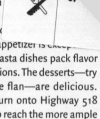

$$$–$$$$ TRADING POST CAFE. A postmodern
★ impeccable service, and an imaginative
Trading Post the most popular dining sp
The perfectly marinated salmon gravlax appetizer is except
and the paella is a bounty for two. The pasta dishes pack flavor
to equal their unbelievably generous portions. The desserts—try
the homemade raspberry sorbet or the flan—are delicious.
Coming from the north, take the left turn onto Highway 518
(Talpa Road) just before the restaurant to reach the more ample
parking lot. Be careful not to walk over the neighbor's yard; to
reach the restaurant's entrance, walk back along Talpa Road.
*4179 Paseo del Pueblo Sur (NM 68), Ranchos de Taos, tel. 505/758–5089.
D, DC, MC, V. Closed Sun.*

ARROYO SECO AND POINTS NORTH
Cafés

$–$$ TAOS COW. This growing enterprise has expanded into the former
Casa Fresen Bakery building. Not only is it the world headquarters
for tasty ice cream made from growth-hormone-free milk (featured
in area health food stores), but the remodeled dining areas have
become a fine spot for coffee, tea, chai, deli items, pastries,
cookies, and fresh-baked bread (such as the tasty zucchini bread).
Favorites among the three-dozen ice cream flavors are cherry
ristra, piñon caramel, and the true test—vanilla. *591 Hondo Seco
Rd., tel. 505/776–5640. MC, V.*

$ ABE'S CANTINA Y COCINA. Have your breakfast burrito, rolled
tacos, or homemade tamales at one of the small tables crowded
next to the canned goods, or take it on a picnic. You never know
when the place might be closed for golf outings. *Taos Ski Valley
Rd. (County Rd. 150), tel. 505/776–8643. No credit cards. Closed Sun.*

Contemporary

,$ MOMENTITOS DE LA VIDA. Opened in early 1999 in the former
★ Casa Cordova, chef Chris Maher's restaurant brings an ambitious,
worldly focus to dining out in the area. There's an outdoor terrace
and a playfully elegant interior (trompe-l'oeil garlands and
fireplace "stonework"), but focus is on the food. An evening's
entrée might be apricot-glazed game hen or or seared salmon in
sun-dried tomato fish stock, but save some room for desserts,
which change nightly. Live music in the piano bar several nights
a week might include smoky-smooth jazz vocals by Mary Bruscini.
Sunday brunch allows those on a tighter budget to enjoy the
food and atmosphere. *Taos Ski Valley Rd. (County Rd. 150), tel. 505/
776–3333. AE, MC, V. Closed Mon. No lunch.*

Italian

$$$$ VILLA FONTANA. Entering this restaurant, which serves northern
★ Italian cuisine, is like walking into a sophisticated Italian country
inn: warm coral walls, candlelight, gleaming hardwood tables,
starched linens, and courtly service. Notable dishes include grilled
whole sole and seasonal game like venison and pheasant. Lunch
is served in the garden. *NM 522, 5 mi north of Taos Plaza, Arroyo Hondo,
tel. 505/758–5800. AE, D, DC, MC, V. Closed Sun. No lunch Nov.–May.*

Southwestern

$$–$$$ TIM'S CHILE CONNECTION. Young skiers flock to this place
between the turn-off for the Taos Ski Valley and Arroyo Seco for
beer, country-western music, and Tim's stick-to-your-ribs
Southwestern blue-corn tortillas, homemade salsa, buffalo burgers
and steaks, and fajitas. The tab is pricey for what you get, but the
margaritas are monumental and even memorable. *Taos Ski Valley
Rd. (County Rd. 150), tel. 505/776–8787. AE, MC, V.*

SHOPPING

Taos Plaza consists mostly of T-shirt emporiums and souvenir shops that are easily bypassed, though a few stores, like Blue Rain Gallery, carry quality Native American artifacts and jewelry. The more upscale galleries and boutiques are two short blocks north on Bent Street, including the John Dunn House Shops. Kit Carson Road, also known as U.S. 64, has a mix of the old and the new. There's metered municipal parking downtown, though the traffic can be daunting. Some shops worth checking out are in St. Francis Plaza in Ranchos de Taos, 4 mi south of the Plaza near the San Francisco de Asís Church.

ART GALLERIES

For at least a century, artists have been drawn to Taos by its special light, open space, and connections to nature. The result is a vigorous art community with some 80 galleries, a lively market, and an estimated 1,000 residents producing art full- or part-time. Many artists explore themes of the Western landscape, Native Americans, and adobe architecture; others create abstract forms and mixed-media works that may or may not reflect the Southwest. Some local artists grew up in Taos, but many—Anglo, Hispanic, and Native Americans—are adopted Taoseños.

Blue Rain Gallery (117 S. Plaza, tel. 505/751–0066) carries some of the finest examples of Pueblo pottery and Hopi katsina dolls to be found anywhere, ranging in price from several hundred to several thousand dollars. The owner, Leroy Garcia, takes time to explain the materials and traditions; you'll learn a great deal during a short visit here. The gallery also sells Indian-made jewelry and art.

Clay and Fiber Gallery (210 Paseo del Pueblo Sur, tel. 505/758–8093) has exhibited first-rate ceramics, glass, pottery, and hand-painted silks and weavings by local artists for the past quarter century.

Fenix Gallery (228-B Paseo del Pueblo Norte, tel. 505/758–9120) is a showcase for contemporary art, exhibiting paintings, sculpture, ceramics, and lithography by established Taos artists.

La Tierra Gallery (124-G Bent St., tel. 505/758–0101) has nature as its featured artist. Fossils and minerals that have been crafted into jewelry and graceful carvings are for sale.

Leo Weaver Jewelry Galleries represents 50 local jewelry artists at two locations (62 St. Francis Plaza, Ranchos de Taos, tel. 505/751–1003; Historic Taos Inn, 125 Paseo del Pueblo Norte, tel. 505/758–8171). You'll find contemporary and traditional designs in silver, gold, and precious stones, as well as beautiful silver disk concha belts.

Lumina Gallery (239 Morada La., tel. 505/758–7282) exhibits paintings solely by artists who have worked in New Mexico for at least 20 years, as well as sculpture, photography, mixed-media pieces, and antiques. Artists represented include Joe Waldrun and Chuck Henningsen. The impressive works decorate the former adobe home of Victor Higgins, one of the original members of the Taos Society of Artists. The outdoor sculpture garden is a serene oasis conducive to lingering, which the owners happily encourage.

Michael McCormick Gallery (106C Paseo del Pueblo Norte, tel. 505/758–1372) is home to the sensual, stylized female portraits by Miguel Martinez and the architectural paintings of Margaret Nes. An important annex is the JD Challenger studio and gallery. JD Challenger is renowned for his paintings of Native Americans.

Mission Gallery (138 E. Kit Carson Rd., tel. 505/758–2861) carries the works of early Taos artists, early New Mexico modernists, and important contemporary artists. The gallery is in the former home of painter Joseph H. Sharp.

Navajo Gallery (210 Ledoux St., tel. 505/758–3250) shows the works of owner and Navajo painter R. C. Gorman, well known for his ethereal interpretations of Indian imagery.

New Directions Gallery (107-B N. Plaza, tel. 505/758–2771 or 800/658–6903) displays works by contemporary Taos artists such as Larry Bell, Ted Egri, and Maya Torres in a light-filled room.

Parks Gallery (140 Kit Carson Rd., tel. 505/751–0343) specializes in contemporary paintings, sculptures, and prints. Mixed-media artist Melissa Zink shows here.

R. B. Ravens Gallery (St. Francis Plaza, Ranchos de Taos, tel. 505/758–7322) exhibits paintings by the founding artists of Taos, pre-1930s weavings, and ceramics.

Shriver Gallery (401 Paseo del Pueblo Norte, tel. 505/758–4994) handles drawings and etchings, traditional bronze sculptures, and paintings, including oils, watercolors, and pastels.

Six Directions (110 S. Plaza, tel. 505/758–4376) has paintings, alabaster and bronze sculpture, Native American artifacts, silver jewelry, and pottery. Bill Rabbit and Robert Redbird are among the artists represented here.

Spirit Runner Gallery (303 Paseo del Pueblo Norte, tel. 505/758–1132) exhibits colorful acrylic and gold-leaf paintings by Taos native Ouray Meyers.

SPECIALTY STORES
Books

Brodsky Bookshop (218 Paseo del Pueblo Norte, tel. 505/758–9468) has books—contemporary literature, Southwestern classics, children's titles—sometimes piled every which way, but the amiable staff will help you find whatever you need.

Fernandez de Taos Book Store (109 N. Plaza, tel. 505/758–4391) carries magazines, major out-of-town newspapers, and many books on Southwestern culture and history.

G. Robinson Old Prints and Maps (John Dunn House, 124D Bent St., tel. 505/758–2278) stocks rare books, Edward Curtis photographs, and maps and prints from the 16th to 19th century.

Merlin's Garden (127 Bent St., tel. 505/758–0985) is a funky repository of metaphysical books and literature from Ram Dass to Thomas More. The shop also carries tapes, incense, crystals, and jewelry.

Moby Dickens (No. 6, John Dunn House, 124A Bent St., tel. 505/758–3050), great for browsing, is a bookstore for all ages. It carries many books on the Southwest.

Mystery Ink (121 Camino de la Placita, tel. 505/751–1092) specializes in high-quality used books, especially murder mysteries. The shop also carries some foreign-language literature.

Taos Book Shop (122D Kit Carson Rd., tel. 505/758–3733), the oldest bookshop in New Mexico, founded in 1947, specializes in out-of-print and Southwestern books. The founders, Genevieve Janssen and Claire Morrill, compiled the reminiscences of their Taos years in the interesting *A Taos Mosaic* (University of New Mexico Press). Book signings and author receptions are frequently held here.

Clothing

Mariposa Boutique (John Dunn House, 120F Bent St., tel. 505/758–9028) sells Southwestern clothing and accessories by leading Taos designers. The store also sells handcrafted jewelry.

Overland Sheepskin Company (NM 522, tel. 505/758–8822; 100-A McCarthy Plaza, tel. 505/758–5150) carries high-quality sheepskin coats, hats, mittens, and slippers, many with Taos beadwork.

Taos Moccasin Co. Factory Outlet (216 Paseo del Pueblo Sur, tel. 505/758–4276) sells moccasins made in the building next door—everything from booties for babies to men's high and low boots. This shop has great discounts and interesting designs.

Home Furnishings

Casa Cristal Pottery (1306 Paseo del Pueblo Norte, tel. 505/758–1530), 2½ mi north of the Taos Plaza, has it all: stoneware, serapes, clay pots, Native American ironwood carvings, straw and tin ornaments, fountains, sweaters, ponchos, clay fireplaces, Mexican blankets, clay churches, birdbaths, baskets, tiles, piñatas, and blue glassware from Guadalajara. Also in stock are wrought-iron antique reproductions.

Country Furnishings of Taos (534 Paseo del Pueblo Norte, tel. 505/758–4633) sells folk art from northern New Mexico; handmade furniture, metalwork lamps and beds; and many other colorful accessories.

Flying Carpet (208 Ranchitos Rd., tel. 505/751–4035) carries colorful rugs and kilims from Turkey, Kurdistan, Persia, and elsewhere. Owner Bill Eagleton, who wrote a book about Kurdish carpets, and his wife, Kay, have a keen eye for quality and design.

Franzetti Metalworks (120G Bent St., tel. 505/758–7872) displays owner Pozzi Franzetti's whimsical steelwork designs—from switch plate covers to wall hangings in animal and Western motifs.

Hacienda de San Francisco (4 St. Francis Plaza, Ranchos de Taos, tel. 505/758–0477) has an exceptional collection of Spanish-colonial antiques.

Lo Fino (201 Paseo del Pueblo Sur, tel. 505/758–0298) carries the works—hand-carved beds, tables, chairs, trasteros (free-standing cupboards), and benches—of the 10 top Southwestern furniture and lighting designers, as well as some Native American alabaster sculpture, basketry, and pottery.

LYNCO Design Pottery (124-C Bent St., tel. 505/758–3601) features the decoratively painted oven ware of Taos artist Lynn FitzGerald. The high-fired, stoneware pottery comes in serving bowls, pie plates, casserole dishes, and other forms to suit your baking needs.

Partridge Company (241 Ledoux St., at Ranchitos Rd., tel. 505/758–1225) sells linens, rugs, woven bedcovers, and accessories. The shop's owner fashions some eye-catching dried-flower arrangements.

Taos Blue (101A Bent St., tel. 505/758–3561) carries jewelry, pottery, and contemporary works by Native Americans (masks, rattles, sculpture), as well as Hispanic santos (bultos and retablos).

The **Taos Company** (124K Bent St., tel. 800/548–1141) sells magnificent Spanish-style furniture, chandeliers, rugs, and textiles; Mexican *equipal* (wood and leather) chairs; and other accessories.

Taos Tinworks (1204 Paseo del Pueblo Norte, tel. 505/758–9724) sells handcrafted tinwork such as wall sconces, mirrors, lamps, and table ornaments by Marion Moore.

Native American Arts and Crafts

Broken Arrow (222 N. Plaza, tel. 505/758–4304) specializes in collector-quality Native American arts and crafts, including sand paintings, rugs, prints, jewelry, pottery, artifacts, and Hopi katsina dolls.

Buffalo Dancer (103A E. Plaza, tel. 505/758–8718) buys, sells, and trades Native American arts and crafts, including pottery, belts, katsina dolls, hides, and silver-coin jewelry.

Don Fernando Curios and Gifts (104 W. Plaza, tel. 505/758–3791), which opened in 1938 (it's the oldest Native American arts shop on the Taos Plaza), sells good turquoise jewelry, katsinas, straw baskets, and colorful beads.

El Rincón (114 E. Kit Carson Rd., tel. 505/758–9188) is housed in a large, dark, cluttered century-old adobe. Native American items of all kinds are bought and sold here: drums, feathered headdresses, Navajo rugs, beads, bowls, baskets, shields, beaded moccasins, jewelry, arrows, and spearheads. The packed back room contains Indian, Hispanic, and Anglo Wild West artifacts.

Southwest Moccasin & Drum (803 Paseo del Pueblo Norte, tel. 505/758–9332 or 800/447–3630) has 716 native moccasin styles and 72 sizes of drums, many painted by local artists.

Taos Drums (Santa Fe Hwy./NM 68, tel. 505/758–3796 or 800/424–3786) is the factory outlet for the Taos Drum Factory. The store, 5 mi south of Taos Plaza (look for the large tepee), stocks handmade Pueblo log drums, leather lamp shades, and wrought-iron and Southwestern furniture.

Taos General Store (223 Paseo del Pueblo Sur, tel. 505/758–9051) represents a good part of the world in the large showroom's selection of furniture and decorative items. You can also wander among the displays of American Indian pots, rugs, and jewelry. Some items are at wholesale prices.

Outdoor Equipment

Los Rios Anglers (226C Paseo del Pueblo Norte, tel. 505/758–2798 or 800/748–1707) is a fly-fisherman's haven for fly rods, flies, clothing, books, instruction, and guide service to local streams.

Mudd 'n' Flood Mountain Shop (134 Bent St., tel. 505/751–9100) has gear and clothing for rock climbers, backpackers, campers, and backcountry skiers.

Taos Mountain Outfitters (114 S. Plaza, tel. 505/758–9292) supplies kayakers, skiers, and backpackers with what they need, as well as maps, books, and handy advice.

OUTDOOR ACTIVITIES AND SPORTS

Whether you plan to cycle around town, jog along Paseo del Pueblo Norte, or play a few rounds of golf, keep in mind that the altitude in Taos is over 7,000 ft. It's best to keep physical exertion to a minimum until your body becomes acclimated to the altitude—a full day to a few days depending on your constitution. With the decreased oxygen and humidity you may experience some or all of the following symptoms: headache, nausea, insomnia, shortness of breath, diarrhea, sleeplessness, and anxiety. If you are planning to engage in physical activity, avoid alcohol and coffee (which aggravate "high-altitude syndrome") and drink a lot of water and juice.

PARTICIPANT SPORTS
Bicycling

Taos-area roads are steep and hilly, and none have marked bicycle lanes, so be careful while cycling. The **Enchanted Circle Wheeler Peak Bicycle Rally** (tel. 800/384–6444) takes place in mid-September. The rally loops through the entire 84-mi Enchanted Circle, through Red River, Taos, Angel Fire, Eagle Nest, and Questa, past a brilliant blaze of fall color. During the summer, you can head up the mountainside via ski lift in Red River, Angel Fire, and Sipapu.

The **West Rim Trail**, a route opened in 1998, offers a fairly flat but view-studded 9-mi ride that follows the Rio Grande canyon's west rim from the Rio Grande Gorge Bridge to near the Taos Junction Bridge.

"Gearing Up" Bicycle Shop (129 Paseo del Pueblo Sur, tel. 505/751–0365) is a full-service bike shop that also has information about tours and guides. **Native Sons Adventures** (715 Paseo del Pueblo Sur, tel. 505/758–9342 or 800/753–7559) offers guided tours on its mountain bikes.

Fishing

Picurís Pueblo and Cabresto Lake in the Carson National Forest have good trout fishing. The Upper Red River valley is good for bait and fly fishing. For trout fishing far off the beaten path try Hopewell Lake, in Carson National Forest, 30 minutes by car from Tres Piedras (35 mi west of Taos). The lake is open from May to October.

In Taos, **Los Rios Anglers** (226C Paseo del Pueblo Norte, tel. 505/758–2798 or 800/748–1707) offers free one-hour fly-casting clinics, weekly between May and August. Well-known area fishing guide **Taylor Streit** (tel. 505/751–1312) also takes individuals or small groups out for fishing and lessons.

Golf

The 18-hole, par-72 course at the **Angel Fire Country Club** (Country Club Dr. off NM 434, Angel Fire, tel. 505/377–3055), one of the highest in the nation, is open from May to mid-October. The greens fee is $35; an optional cart costs $12.50 per person.

The greens fee at the 18-hole, PGA-rated, par-72 championship course at **Taos Country Club** (Hwy. 570, Ranchos de Taos, tel. 505/758–7300) ranges between $25 and $42; optional carts cost $22.

Health Clubs & Fitness Centers

The **Northside Health & Fitness Center** (1307 Paseo del Pueblo Norte, tel. 505/751–1242) is a spotlessly clean facility with indoor and outdoor pools, a hot tub, tennis courts, and aerobics classes. Nonmembers pay $9 per day; passes for a week or longer are also available. The center provides paid child care with a certified Montessori teacher.

About 3 mi south of the Plaza, **Taos Spa & Tennis Club** (111 Doña Ana Dr., tel. 888/758–1981) has tennis and racquetball courts, indoor and outdoor pools, fitness equipment, saunas, steam rooms, and hot tubs, as well as baby-sitting and massage services. Nonmembers pay $10 per day. The **Taos Youth and Family Center** (105 Camino de Colores, tel. 505/758–4160) has an outdoor Olympic-size ice arena, where rollerblading, volleyball, and basketball take place in summer. Other scheduled activities are open to the public.

Hiking

Strenuous trails from the Village of Taos Ski Valley lead to **Wheeler Peak,** the highest point in New Mexico, at 13,161 ft. Gentler paths head up other piney and meadow-filled mountains like **Gold Hill.** There are also trails in the valley that pass by old mining camps. For canyon climbing, head into the wooded Italiano on the way to the Taos Ski Valley, or the rocky **Rio Grande Gorge.** The best entry point into the gorge is at the Wild Rivers Recreation Area in Cerro, 35 mi north of Taos.

Visitors from lower altitudes should take time to acclimatize, and all hikers should follow basic safety procedures. Wind, cold, and wetness can occur any time of year, and the mountain climate produces sudden storms. Dress in layers; carry water, food, sunscreen, hat, sunglasses, and a first-aid kit; and wear sturdy footwear. Maps and information about trails are available from the **U.S. Forest Service** (208 Cruz Alta, Taos, tel. 505/758–6200); the **Bureau of Land Management, Taos Resource Area Office** (226 Cruz Alta, Taos, tel. 505/758–8851); and local outfitters (☞ Outdoor Equipment in Shopping, *above*).

River Rafting

The **Taos Box,** at the bottom of the steep-walled canyon far below the Rio Grande Gorge Bridge, is the granddaddy of thrilling white water in New Mexico and is best attempted by experts only—or on a guided trip—but the river also offers more placid sections such as through the Orilla Verde Recreation Area. Spring runoff is the busy season, from mid-April through June, but rafting companies conduct tours March to November. Shorter two-hour options usually cover the fairly tame section of the river. The Bureau of Land Management, Taos Resource Area Office has a list of registered river guides and information about running the river on your own.

Far Flung Adventures (15 State Highway 522, El Prado, tel. 505/758–2628 or 800/359–2627) operates half-day, full-day, and overnight rafting trips along the Rio Grande and the Rio Chama.

Kokopelli Rafting Adventures (541 Cordova Rd., Santa Fe, tel. 800/879–9035) takes you through the Taos Box or down other stretches of the river.

Los Rios River Runners (Taos, tel. 800/544–1181) will take you to your choice of spots—the Rio Chama, the Lower Gorge, or the Taos Box.

Native Sons Adventures (715 Paseo del Pueblo Sur, tel. 505/758–9342 or 800/753–7559) offers several trip options on the Rio Grande.

Running

The track around the football field at **Taos High School** (134 Cervantes St., tel. 505/758–5230) isn't officially open to the public, but no one seems to object when nonstudents jog there. The paved paths and grass of **Kit Carson Memorial Park** make for a pleasant run. The mountain roads north of Taos present a formidable challenge.

Skiing

RESORTS

The five ski resorts within 90 mi of Taos have beginning, intermediate, and advanced slopes and snowmobile and cross-country skiing trails. All the resorts have fine accommodations and safe child-care programs at reasonable prices. Only Taos Ski Valley prohibits snowboarding.

Angel Fire Resort (N. Angel Fire Rd. off NM 434, Angel Fire, tel. 505/377–6401; 800/633–7463 outside NM) has a hotel and is open from mid-December to the first week in April.

Red River Ski Area (Pioneer Rd. off NM 38, Red River, tel. 505/754–2382) is open from Thanksgiving to Easter.

Sipapu Lodge and Ski Area (NM 518, Vadito, tel. 505/587–2240) is open from mid-December to the end of March.

Ski Rio (NM 196 off NM 522, Costillo, tel. 505/758–7707), north of Taos Ski Valley, opens for daily business from mid-December to early April. The resort has 83 runs and makes its own snow.

Village of Taos Ski Valley (Taos Ski Valley Rd./County Rd. 150, Village of Taos Ski Valley 87525, tel. 505/776–2291 for ski information and ticket office; 505/776–2233 or 800/776–1111 for lodging reservations) is open from late November until the first week in April. This world-class area is known for its alpine village atmosphere, perhaps the finest ski school in the country, and the variety of its 72 runs—51% expert (the ridge chutes, Al's Run, Inferno), 25% intermediate (Honeysuckle), 24% beginner (Bambi, Porcupine). Taos Ski Valley averages 323 inches of annual snowfall and makes its own if needed. There's no snowboarding.

CROSS-COUNTRY

Carson National Forest (Forest Service Building, 208 Cruz Alta Rd., Taos 87571, tel. 505/758–6200) has a good self-guided map of cross-country trails throughout the park. You can drive into the forest land via Highways 522, 150, 38, and 578.

At the **Enchanted Forest Cross-Country Ski Area** (Box 521, Red River 87558, tel. 505/754–2374), 24 mi of groomed trails loop through meadows and pines from the warming hut; the season runs from the end of November to Easter.

Swimming

The **Don Fernando Municipal Swimming Pool** (124 Civic Plaza Dr., tel. 505/758–9171) is open on weekdays from 1 to 4:30 and on weekends from 1 to 5. Admission is $2.

Tennis

Kit Carson Memorial Park (Paseo del Pueblo Norte at Civic Plaza Dr.) and **Fred Baca Park** (301 Camino de Medio) have free public tennis courts, available on a first-come, first-served basis. The **Quail Ridge Inn and Tennis Ranch** (Taos Ski Valley Rd./County Rd. 150, tel. 800/624–4448) has eight Laykold tennis courts (two indoor). Outdoor courts are free to guests; indoor courts cost $15 per hour, $30 per hour for visitors. **Taos Spa & Tennis Club** (111 Doña Ana Dr., tel. 888/758–1981) has tennis and racquetball courts; nonmembers pay $10 per day.

SPECTATOR SPORTS

Spectator sports in the Taos area include the **Rodeo de Taos,** which takes place at the Taos County Rodeo Fairgrounds in mid-June, and the **Taos Mountain Balloon Rally,** held in a field south of downtown during the last week in October. Contact the Taos County Chamber of Commerce (☞ Visitor Information in Practical Information) for more information. **Paradise Balloons** (tel. 505/751–6098) and **Pueblo Balloons** (tel. 505/751–9877) conduct balloon rides over and into the Rio Grande Gorge at sunrise. The cost is $195 plus gratuities.

NIGHTLIFE AND THE ARTS

Evening entertainment is modest in Taos. Some motels and hotels present solo musicians or small combos in their bars and lounges. Everything from down-home blues bands to Texas two-step dancing blossoms on Saturday and Sunday nights in winter. In summer things heat up during the week as well. For information about what's going on around town pick up *Taos Magazine*. The weekly *Taos News*, published on Thursday, carries arts and entertainment information in the "Tempo" section.

NIGHTLIFE
Bars and Lounges

The **Adobe Bar** (Taos Inn, 125 Paseo del Pueblo Norte, tel. 505/758–2233), a local meet-and-greet spot, books talented acts, from solo guitarists to small folk groups, and, two or three nights a week, jazz musicians.

Fernando's Hideaway (Holiday Inn, 1005 Paseo del Pueblo Sur, tel. 505/758–4444) occasionally presents live entertainment— rock, jazz, blues, vocals, and country music. Saturday is reserved for karaoke. Lavish complimentary happy-hour buffets are laid out on weekday evenings. **Weasel Mahood's Bar and Bistro** (122 Paseo del Pueblo Sur, 2nd floor, tel. 505/758–1778) often has dancing, karoke, or live music as well as pool, 10 beers on tap, and the house special, the Weasel Mahood martini.

Cabaret

The **Kachina Lodge Cabaret** (413 Paseo del Pueblo Norte, tel. 505/758–2275) brings in headline acts, such as Arlo Guthrie and the Kingston Trio, on a regular basis and has dancing.

Coffeehouse

Caffe Tazza (122 Kit Carson Rd., tel. 505/758–8706) presents free evening performances throughout the week—folk singing, jazz, blues, poetry, and fiction readings.

Country-and-Western Club

The **Sagebrush Inn** (1508 Paseo del Pueblo Sur, tel. 505/758–2254) hosts musicians and dancing in its lobby lounge. If you hear that South by Southwest is playing, go ahead and check the three-guy band out. There's no cover charge, and if you show up on a Thursday, you can learn to two-step.

Jazz and Dance Clubs

Alley Cantina (121 Teresina La., tel. 505/758–2121) has jazz, folk, and blues—as well as shuffleboard and board games for those not moved to dance. The piano bar at **Momentitos de la Vida** (County Rd. 150 in Arroyo Seco, tel. 505/776–3333) often presents jazz and bossa nova.

At **Tim's Chile Connection** (County Rd. 150, tel. 505/776–2969) on the way to Arroyo Seco, look for lively swing and singers strumming acoustic guitar. **Thunderbird Lodge** (3 Thunderbird Rd., tel. 505/776–2280) in the Taos Ski Valley has free jazz nights and country-and-western swing dancing.

THE ARTS

Summer music has become a staple in Taos, which benefits from talented performers who enjoy coming to the desert-mountain setting. But more spring and fall festivals, spurred by availability of lodgings and venues, are coming to town to enliven slow seasons, too.

The **Taos Art Association** (133 Paseo del Pueblo Norte, tel. 505/758–2052) has information about art-related events in Taos. The **Taos Community Auditorium** (145 Paseo del Pueblo Norte, tel. 505/758–4677) presents plays, dance, concerts, and movies.

Festivals

For information about festivals in Taos, contact the **Taos County Chamber of Commerce** (☞ Visitor Information in Practical Information).

The **Taos Spring Arts Festival,** held throughout Taos in early May, is a showcase for the visual, performing, and literary arts of the community and allows you to rub elbows with the many artists who call Taos home. The Mother's Day Arts and Crafts weekend during the festival always draws a crowd.

Held every year during the second weekend of July, the **Taos Pueblo Powwow** attracts Native Americans from across the country for traditional dances, socializing, and a market on Pueblo land.

The **Taos Fall Arts Festival,** from late September to early October, is the major arts gathering, when buyers are in town and many other events, such as a Taos Pueblo feast, take place.

On the heels of the Fall Arts Festival comes the **Wool Festival** in early October, held in Kit Carson Memorial Park, which celebrates everything from sheep to shawl, with demonstrations of shearing, spinning, and weaving; handmade woolen items for sale; and tastings of favorite lamb dishes.

Film

Taos Talking Picture Festival (tel. 505/751–0637) is a multicultural celebration of cinema artists, with a focus on Native American film and video makers. The mid-April festival presents independent films, documentaries, animation, and some classic cinema.

Music

From mid-June to early August the Taos School of Music and the International Institute of Music fill the evenings with the sounds of chamber and symphonic orchestras at the **Taos Chamber Music Festival** (tel. 505/776–2388). Nearly four decades old, this is America's oldest chamber music summer program and possibly the largest assembly of professional musicians in the Southwest. Concerts are presented every Saturday evening, and every other Friday evening from mid-June to August, at the Taos Community Auditorium. Tickets cost $15. The events at Taos Ski Valley are free.

The Taos School of Music gives free weekly summer concerts and recitals from mid-June to early August at the **Hotel Saint Bernard** (tel. 505/776–2251), at the mountain base (near the lifts) of Taos Ski Valley.

Music from Angel Fire (tel. 505/758–4667 or 505/377–3233) is a series of classical and jazz concerts presented at the Taos Community Auditorium and the Angel Fire Community Auditorium in the town center from August 21 to September 2. Tickets cost about $12 per concert.

WHERE TO STAY

The hotels and motels along NM 68 (Paseo del Pueblo Sur and Norte) suit every need and budget; rates vary little between big-name chains and smaller establishments. Make advance reservations and expect higher rates during the ski season (usually from late December to early April) and in the summer.

The best deals in town are the bed-and-breakfasts. Mostly family-owned, they provide personal service, delicious breakfasts, and many extras that hotels charge for. The B&Bs are often in old adobes that have been refurbished with style and flair. For price categories, *see* the chart *under* Lodging *in* Practical Information.

DOWNTOWN TAOS

$$$–$$$$ CASA DE LAS CHIMENEAS. Regional art, tile hearths, French
★ doors, and traditional viga ceilings are among the design elements of note at the House of Chimneys B&B, 2½ blocks from the Plaza and secluded behind thick walls. Each room in the 1912 structure has a private entrance, a fireplace, handmade New Mexican furniture, and a tile bar stocked with complimentary juices, sodas, and mineral waters. All rooms overlook the gardens and fountains. The two-course breakfasts might include cheese-filled crepes with fresh berries, and late-afternoon hors-d'oeuvres are generous

taos lodging

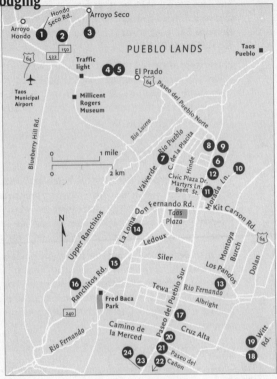

enough to be a light meal. You can also pamper yourself with a massage or spa treatments. *405 Cordoba Rd. (Box 5303), 87571, tel. 505/758–4777 or 800/758–4777, fax 505/758–3976. 8 rooms, 2 suites. In-room VCRs, outdoor hot tub, sauna, exercise room, laundry service. No smoking. AE, MC, V. BP. www.visittaos.com*

$$$–$$$$ **FECHIN INN.** This graceful Pueblo Revival structure on the grounds of the Fechin Institute (to which guests have free admission) is adjacent to Kit Carson Memorial Park. Painter Nicolai Fechin's daughter, Eya, participated in the planning; Fechin reproductions adorn the rooms and hallways, and the woodwork in the large, comfortable lobby is based on the artist's designs. A generous breakfast is available every morning in the lobby, as are cocktails in the evening. Rooms are comfortable, if nondescript; most have private balconies or patios. Pets are welcome. *227 Paseo del Pueblo Norte, 87571, tel. 505/751–1000 or 800/811–2933, fax 505/751–7338. 71 rooms, 14 suites. Massage, exercise room, ski storage, meeting rooms, free parking. AE, D, DC, MC, V. CP. www.fechin-inn.com*

$$$–$$$$ **HISTORIC TAOS INN.** Mere steps from Taos Plaza, this hotel is listed on the National Register of Historic Places. The guest rooms are pleasant and comfortable, and in summer there's dining alfresco on the patio. The lobby, which also serves as seating for the Adobe Bar, is built around an old town well from which a fountain bubbles forth. Many shops and eateries are within walking distance of the inn, and its own restaurant, Doc Martin's (☞ *Eating Out, above*), is quite popular itself. *125 Paseo del Pueblo Norte, 87571, tel. 505/758–2233 or 800/826–7466, fax 505/758–5776. 36 rooms. Restaurant, bar, lounge, library. AE, DC, MC, V. www.taosinn.com*

$$–$$$$ **CASA EUROPA.** The original adobe bricks and wood viga ceiling enhance the pastoral feeling of this classic estate on six acres with views of pastures and mountains. European antiques and Southwestern pieces decorate the rooms of the B&B. Though parts are 200 years old, the two main guest areas are light and airy with comfortable chairs to relax in while the fireplace crackles. Breakfasts are elaborate, and complimentary homemade afternoon pastries are served daily except during the ski season, when they're replaced by evening hors d'oeuvres. 840 Upper Ranchitos Rd., HC 68 (Box 3F), 87571, tel. 888/758–9798, tel./fax 505/758–9798. 7 rooms. 2 lounges, hot tub, sauna. AE, MC, V. BP. www.travelbase.com/destinations/taos/casa.europa

$$–$$$$ HACIENDA DEL SOL. Art patron Mabel Dodge Luhan bought this
★ house in the 1920s and lived here with her husband, Tony Luhan, while building their main house, Las Palomas de Taos. It was also their private retreat and guest house for visiting notables; Frank Waters wrote *People of the Valley* here. Most of the rooms contain kiva-style fireplaces, Southwestern-style handcrafted furniture, and original artwork. The secluded outdoor hot tub has a crystalline view of Taos Mountain. The jet-black bathroom of the Los Amantes Room is a celebration in decadence with its huge black hot tub amid a jungle of potted plants below a skylight. Breakfast is a gourmet affair. Each room has two phone lines. 109 Mabel Dodge La. (Box 177), 87571, tel. 505/758–0287, fax 505/758–5895. 11 rooms. Outdoor hot tub. MC, V. BP. www.taoshaciendadelsol.com

$$–$$$$ INN ON LA LOMA PLAZA. The walls surrounding this Pueblo
★ Revival building (formerly the Taos Hacienda Inn) date from the early 1800s and were designed to protect a small enclave of settlers from Indian attacks. The inn is listed on the National Register of Historic Places and behind it lies the historic, residential La Loma Plaza. The individually decorated rooms have Southwestern accents, including kiva fireplaces and bathrooms with Mexican tile work. The comfortable living room holds an interesting collection of antique cameras and a well-stocked library with books on Taos and art. Owners Jerry and Peggy Davis unobtrusively provide helpful advice about the area and serve a generous breakfast, afternoon snacks, and evening coffee daily. B&B guests also have privileges at the nearby health club (but there's an outdoor hot tub here too). 315 Ranchitos Rd. (Box 4159),

87571, tel. 505/758–1717 or 800/530–3040, fax 505/751–0155. 5
rooms, 2 artist studios with kitchenettes. Hot tub, library. AE, D, MC, V.
BP. www.vacationtaos.com

\$\$–\$\$\$\$ MABEL DODGE LUHAN HOUSE. This National Historic Landmark
was once the home of the heiress who drew the literati to the area.
Guests from pre-B&B days included D. H. and Frieda Lawrence,
Georgia O'Keeffe, and Willa Cather. The main house has nine guest
rooms, and there are eight more in a separate guest house, as
well as a two-bedroom cottage. The inn is frequently used for
literary, artistic, cultural, and educational meetings and workshops.
Don't expect glamour—this is one of the most basic B&Bs in
town. The buildings have been freshened up with new paint and
baths, but the stairs still creak comfortingly. Meal service is
available for groups, and public tennis courts are nearby. 240
Morada La. (Box 3400), 87571, tel. 505/758–9456 or 800/846–2235,
fax 505/751–0431. 15 rooms with bath, 2 with shared bath; 1 cottage.
Meeting rooms. AE, MC, V. BP. www.unink.com/mabel

\$\$–\$\$\$\$ TOUCHSTONE INN. D. H. Lawrence visited this house when
★ Miriam DeWitt owned it in 1929. The inn's owner, Taos artist Bren
Price, has filled the rooms, named after famous Taos literary
figures, with tasteful antique and modern pieces. The grounds
overlook part of the Taos Pueblo lands, and this makes for a quiet
stay within a mile of Taos Plaza. Some suites have fireplaces.
Early-morning coffee is poured in the living room, and breakfasts
with inventive presentations are served in the glassed-in patio.
110 Mabel Dodge La. (Box 2896), 87571, tel. 505/758–0192 or 800/
758–0192, fax 505/758–3498. 8 rooms. In-room VCRs, hot tub. MC, V.
BP. www.touchstoneinn.com

\$\$\$ RAMADA INN DE TAOS. More Taos than Ramada, the two-story
adobe-style hotel welcomes you with a lobby fireplace, desert
colors, Western art, and Native American pottery. The rooms
have an inviting Southwestern flavor as does the new dining
menu. 615 Paseo del Pueblo Sur, 87571, tel. 505/758–2900 or 800/

659–8267, fax 505/758–1662. 124 rooms. Dining room, lounge, indoor pool, hot tub, meeting rooms. AE, D, DC, MC, V.

$$–$$$ BEST WESTERN KACHINA LODGE DE TAOS. Down the road from Taos Pueblo and minutes from the Taos Plaza, this hotel is in a two-story Pueblo-style adobe. From Memorial Day to Labor Day a troupe from Taos Pueblo performs nightly ritual dances outside by firelight. The katsina theme (a doll representing a masked ancestral spirit) is carried throughout, and guest rooms continue the Native American motif with handmade and hand-painted furnishings and colorful bedspreads. 413 Paseo del Pueblo Norte (Box NN), 87571, tel. 505/758–2275 or 800/522–4462, fax 505/758–9207. 113 rooms, 5 suites. Restaurant, bar, coffee shop, pool, hot tub, shops, meeting rooms. AE, D, DC, MC, V. www.kachinalodge.com

$$–$$$ BROOKS STREET INN. An elaborately carved corbel arch, the handiwork of Japanese carpenter Yaichikido, spans the entrance to a shaded, walled garden. Fluffy pillows, fresh flowers, and paintings by local artists are among the grace notes in the rooms. Blue-corn pancakes with pineapple salsa, stuffed French toast with an apricot glaze, and other home-baked delights are served at breakfast, along with coffee or espresso drinks. In warm weather, breakfast is served at umbrella-shaded tables on the patio; in winter it's served by the fireplace. 119 Brooks St. (Box 4954), 87571, tel. 505/ 758–1489 or 800/758–1489. 6 rooms. No smoking. AE, MC, V. BP. www.brooksstreetinn.com

$$–$$$ COMFORT SUITES. Each unit at this complex contains a living room with a sofa bed, a bedroom with a king- and a queen-size bed, a television in both rooms, a microwave oven, a coffeemaker, and a refrigerator. 1500 Paseo del Pueblo Sur (Box 1268), 87571, tel. 505/ 751–1555 or 888/751–1555. 60 suites. In-room data ports, refrigerators, hot tub, pool. AE, D, DC, MC, V. BP.

$$–$$$ HOLIDAY INN DON FERNANDO DE TAOS. The accommodations at this hotel with a Pueblo-style design are grouped around central courtyards and connected by walkways. Appointed with hand-carved New Mexican furnishings, the rooms have kiva-style fireplaces. There's a free shuttle to take guests to the town center. *1005 Paseo del Pueblo Sur, 87571, tel. 505/758–4444 or 800/759–2736, fax 505/758–0055. 124 rooms. Restaurant, bar, lounge, pool, hot tub, tennis court. AE, D, DC, MC, V. www.taoswebb.com/holidayinn/*

$$–$$$ LA POSADA DE TAOS. A couple of blocks from Taos Plaza, this provincial adobe has beam ceilings, a portal, and the intimacy of a private hacienda. Five of the guest rooms are in the main house; the sixth is a separate cottage with a queen-size four-poster bed, a sitting room, and a fireplace—a setting cozy and pretty enough to earn the name *La Casa de la Luna de Miel* (The Honeymoon House). The rooms have mountain views or face a flowering courtyard; all but one of the rooms have adobe, kiva-style fireplaces. Breakfasts are hearty. *309 Juanita La. (Box 1118), 87571, tel. 505/758–8164 or 800/645–4803, fax 505/751–4694. 5 rooms, 1 cottage. AE, MC, V. BP.*

$$–$$$ OLD TAOS GUESTHOUSE. Once a ramshackle adobe hacienda, this homey B&B has been completely and lovingly outfitted with the owners' hand-carved doors and furniture, Western artifacts, and antiques. Some rooms have the smallest bathrooms you'll ever encounter but have private entrances and some have fireplaces. There are 80-mi views from the outdoor hot tub and it's just a five-minute drive to town. The owners welcome families. Breakfasts are healthy and hearty. *1028 Witt Rd. (Box 6552), 87571, tel. 800/758–5448, tel./fax 505/758–5448. 9 rooms. Hot tub. MC, V. BP.*

$$–$$$ ORINDA. Built in 1947, this adobe estate has spectacular views and country privacy. The one- and two-bedroom suites have separate entrances, kiva-style fireplaces, traditional viga ceilings, and Mexican-tile baths. Two rooms share a common sitting room. One suite has a Jacuzzi. The hearty breakfast is served family-style in the soaring two-story sun atrium amid a gallery of artworks, all for sale. *461 Valverde (Box 4451), 87571, tel. 505/758–8581 or 800/*

847–1837, fax 505/751–4895. 5 rooms. No smoking. AE, MC, V. BP.
www.taosnet.com/orinda

$$–$$$ SAN GERONIMO LODGE. On a small street off Kit Carson Road,
this lodge built in 1925 sits on 2½ acres that front majestic Taos
Mountain and back up to the Carson National Forest. A balcony
library, attractive grounds, many rooms with fireplaces, two
rooms designed for people with disabilities, and a room for guests
with a pet are among the draws. The hotel staff will arrange ski
packages. 1101 Witt Rd., 87571, tel. 505/751–3776 or 800/894–4119,
fax 505/751–1493. 18 rooms. Pool, hot tub, massage. AE, D, DC, MC, V.

$$ EL PUEBLO LODGE. This low-to-the-ground, pueblo-style adobe
a few blocks north of Taos Plaza has practical in-room amenities
and guest laundry rooms. The traditional Southwestern furnishings
and fireplaces lend the rooms a homey feel. 412 Paseo del Pueblo
Norte (Box 92), 87571, tel. 505/758–8700 or 800/433–9612, fax 505/
758–7321. 61 rooms. Kitchenettes, refrigerators, pool, hot tub, coin
laundry. AE, D, MC, V. CP. www.taoswebb.com/hotel/elpueblo

SAGEBRUSH INN. A tad run-down but still with a certain allure,
this Pueblo Mission–style 1929 adobe 3 mi south of the Plaza
contains authentic Navajo rugs, rare pottery, Southwestern and
Spanish antiques, fine carved pieces, and paintings by
Southwestern masters. Georgia O'Keeffe once lived and painted
in one of the third-story rooms. Many of the bedrooms have kiva-
style fireplaces; some have balconies looking out to the Sangre
de Cristo Mountains. There's country-western music nightly. The
Sagebrush Village offers condominium family lodging, too. 1508
Paseo del Pueblo Sur (Box 557), 87571, tel. 505/758–2254 or 800/428–
3626, fax 505/758–5077. 68 rooms, 32 suites. 2 restaurants, bar,
lounge, pool, 2 hot tubs, meeting rooms. AE, D, DC, MC, V.
www.sagebrushinn.com

$–$$$ SUN GOD LODGE. Though inexpensive, this motel has old adobe
charm with basic amenities—it's a good deal. Right on the main
highway, the Sun God is convenient to restaurants and historic

sites. *909 Paseo del Pueblo Sur, 87571, tel. 505/758–3162 or 800/821–2437, fax 505/758–1716. 55 rooms. Hot tub. AE, D, MC, V. www.sungodlodge.com*

RANCHOS DE TAOS

$$–$$$$ **ADOBE & PINES INN.** Native American and Mexican artifacts decorate the main house of this B&B, which has expansive mountain views. Part of the main building dates from 1830. The rooms contain Mexican-tiled baths, kiva fireplaces, fluffy goose-down pillows, and comforters. A separate cottage and two equally handsome casitas also house guests. The owners serve gourmet breakfasts in a sunny glass-enclosed patio. *NM 68 and Llano Quemado (Box 837), Ranchos de Taos 87557, tel. 505/751–0947 or 800/723–8267, fax 505/758–8423. 5 rooms, 1 cottage, 2 casitas. 5 hot tubs, sauna. No smoking. AE, MC, V. BP. www.taosnet.com/adobepines*

ARROYO SECO

$$$–$$$$ **QUAIL RIDGE INN RESORT.** On the way to Taos Ski Valley, this large resort has one- and two-story modern adobe bungalows that are comfy and efficient. Some suites have kitchens. The resort provides a host of recreational amenities, from organized trail rides to hot-tub soaks. Skiing, tennis, rafting, mountain-biking, and fly-fishing packages are available for groups or individuals. *Taos Ski Valley Rd. (County Rd. 150; Box 707), Taos 87571, tel. 505/776–2211 or 800/624–4448, fax 505/776–2949. 50 rooms, 60 suites. Restaurant, lounge, in-room data ports, pool, hot tub, 8 tennis courts, exercise room, racquetball, squash, volleyball, meeting rooms. AE, D, DC, MC, V. www.taoswebb.com/hotel/quailridge*

$$$–$$$$ **CASA GRANDE GUEST RANCH.** Watch the stars and the lights of Taos twinkle from the hot tub of this B&B; morning views stretch for miles. Three comfortable rooms are integrated into the family home built not far from the property's historic hacienda on the flanks of El Salto Mountain. Breakfast burritos with all the trimmings will see you through a horseback ride up to the

Not a Night Owl?

You can learn a lot about a place if you take its pulse after dark. So even if you're the original early-to-bed type, there's every reason to vary your routine when you're away from home.

EXPERIENCE THE FAMILIAR IN A NEW PLACE Whether your thing is going to the movies or going to concerts, it's always different away from home. In clubs, new faces and new sounds add up to a different scene. Or you may catch movies you'd never see at home.

TRY SOMETHING NEW Do something you've never done before. It's another way to dip into the local scene. A simple suggestion: Go out later than usual—go dancing late and finish up with breakfast at dawn.

DO SOMETHING OFFBEAT Look into lectures and readings as well as author appearances in book stores. You may even meet your favorite novelist.

EXPLORE A DAYTIME NEIGHBORHOOD AT NIGHT Take a nighttime walk through an explorable area you've already seen by day. You'll get a whole different view of it.

ASK AROUND If you strike up a conversation with like-minded people during the course of your day, ask them about their favorite spots. Your hotel concierge is another resource.

DON'T WING IT As soon as you've nailed down your travel dates, look into local publications or surf the Net to see what's on the calendar while you're in town. Look for hot regional acts, dance and theater, big-name performing artists, expositions, and sporting events. Then call or click to order tickets.

CHECK OUT THE NEIGHBORHOOD Whenever you don't know the neighborhood you'll be visiting, review safety issues with people in your hotel. What's the transportation situation? Can you walk there, or do you need a cab? Is there anything else you need to know?

CASH OR CREDIT? Know before you go. It's always fun to be surprised—but not when you can't cover your check.

waterfalls. Guests must be 18 and over. *75 Luis O. Torres Rd., Arroyo Seco 87514, tel. 888/236–1303, fax 505/776–2177. 3 rooms. Hot tub. AE, MC, V. BP. www.guestranch.com*

$$–$$$$ ALMA DEL MONTE. Mountain views abound from the rooms and the courtyard of this B&B on the high plain between Taos and the ski valley. Saltillo-tiled floors, Victorian antiques, canopies over some of the beds, generous breakfasts, and afternoon wine with hors d'oeuvres make it a hard place to leave, even for skiing. *372 Hondo Seco Rd. (Box 1434), Taos 87571, tel. 505/776–2721 or 800/273–7203, fax 505/776–8888. 5 rooms. MC, V. BP. www.almadelmonte-bb.com/spirit*

CAMPGROUNDS

⚠ Orilla Verde Recreation Area. You can hike, fish, and picnic at this area along the banks of the Rio Grande, 10 mi south of Ranchos de Taos, off NM 68 at NM 570. As for paying the camping fee, leave cash in an envelope provided, drop it in a tube, and the rangers will collect it. *Mailing address: Bureau of Land Management, Cruz Alta Rd., Taos 87571, tel. 505/758–8851. 70 tent sites. Rest rooms. No credit cards.*

⚠ Taos RV Park. The sites are grassy, with a few small trees, in this park 3¼ mi from Taos Plaza near the junction of NM 68 and NM 518. A recreation room has video games, TV, and a pool table. Some RV supplies are for sale. There are rest rooms and hot showers. *1799 Paseo del Pueblo Sur, next to the Taos Motel (Box 729F), Ranchos de Taos 87557, tel. 505/758–1667 or 800/323–6009. 29 RV and tent sites. Kitchenette, horseshoes, billiards, recreation room, playground. D, MC, V.*

PRACTICAL INFORMATION

Air Travel

BOOKING

When you book **look for nonstop flights** and **remember that "direct" flights stop at least once.** Try to avoid connecting flights, which require a change of plane.

CARRIERS

Once you've landed in one of New Mexico's two gateways, Albuquerque or El Paso, Texas, you can take advantage of some regional airlines. Mesa Airlines offers shuttle flights to larger communities in the state including Las Cruces and Roswell. Rio Grande Air operates daily flights between Albuquerque and Taos. Charter flights also are available. Costs are significantly higher per air mile when you venture off a major air carrier onto a shuttle or charter flight with fewer passengers, but you can weigh those costs against convenience. Since choices are few, you are unlikely to find airfare bargains once you leave a major airport.

➤ MAJOR AIRLINES: **American** (tel. 800/433–7300). **Continental** (tel. 800/525–0280). **Delta** (tel. 800/221–1212). **Northwest** (tel. 800/692–7000). **TWA** (tel. 800/221–2000). **United** (tel. 800/241–6522). **US Airways** (tel. 800/428–4322).

➤ SMALLER AIRLINES: **America West** (tel. 800/235–9292). **Frontier** (tel. 800/432–1359). **Mesa Airlines** (tel. 800/637–2247). **Rio Grande Air** (tel. 877/435–9742). **Southwest Airlines** (tel. 800/435–9792).

➤ FROM THE U.K.: **British Airways** (tel. 0345/222–111). **Delta** (tel. 0800/414–767). **United Airlines** (tel. 0800/888–555).

CUTTING COSTS

The least expensive airfares to New Mexico must usually be purchased in advance and are nonrefundable. It's smart to **call a number of airlines, and when you are quoted a good price,**

book it on the spot—the same fare may not be available the next day. Always **check different routings** and look into using different airports. Travel agents, especially low-fare specialists, are helpful.

Consolidators are another good source. They buy tickets for scheduled international flights at reduced rates from the airlines, then sell them at prices that beat the best fare available directly from the airlines, usually without restrictions. Sometimes you can even get your money back if you need to return the ticket. Carefully read the fine print detailing penalties for changes and cancellations, and **confirm your consolidator reservation with the airline.**

➤ CONSOLIDATORS: **Cheap Tickets** (tel. 800/377–1000). **Discount Airline Ticket Service** (tel. 800/576–1600). **Unitravel** (tel. 800/325–2222). **Up & Away Travel** (tel. 212/889–2345). **World Travel Network** (tel. 800/409–6753).

HOW TO COMPLAIN

If your baggage goes astray or your flight goes awry, complain right away. Most carriers require that you **file a claim immediately.**

➤ AIRLINE COMPLAINTS: U.S. Department of Transportation **Aviation Consumer Protection Division** (C-75, Room 4107, Washington, DC 20590, tel. 202/366–2220, www.dot.gov/airconsumer). **Federal Aviation Administration Consumer Hotline** (tel. 800/322–7873).

Airports

The major gateway to Santa Fe and Taos is Albuquerque International Sunport, which grants quick access to Albuquerque but is still 65 mi southwest of Santa Fe and 130 mi south of Taos. There is no regular air service between Albuquerque and Santa Fe. Rio Grande Air offers several round-trips daily between Albuquerque and Taos Municipal Airport, 12 mi west of the city.

➤ **AIRPORT INFORMATION: Albuquerque International Sunport** (Sunport Blvd. off I–25, 5 mi south of downtown, tel. 505/842–4366). **Santa Fe Municipal Airport** (Airport Rd./NM 284 west of NM 14, tel. 505/473–7243). **Taos Municipal Airport** (U.S. 64, 12 mi west of Taos, tel. 505/758–4995).

TRANSFERS

Shuttle buses between the Albuquerque International Sunport and Santa Fe take about 1 hour and 20 minutes and cost approximately $20 each way. Shuttle service between Albuquerque and Taos takes 2¾ hours and costs $30–$35. Reservations are advised on all shuttles. Ask about round-trip and group discounts.

➤ **BETWEEN ALBUQUERQUE AND SANTA FE: Express Shuttle USA** (tel. 800/256–8991). **Sandia Shuttle Express** (tel. 505/474–5696).

➤ **BETWEEN ALBUQUERQUE AND TAOS: Faust's Transportation** (tel. 505/758–7359). **Pride of Taos** (tel. 505/758–8340). **Twin Hearts Express** (tel. 505/751–1201).

Bus Travel

Bus service on Texas, New Mexico & Oklahoma Coaches, affiliated with Greyhound Lines, is available between major cities and towns in New Mexico. A one-way ticket from Albuquerque to Santa Fe costs about $12; to Taos, about $22. Make reservations several weeks in advance of major holidays or other special events such as the Kodak Albuquerque International Balloon Fiesta in October.

➤ **BUS INFORMATION: Greyhound** (858 St. Michael's Dr., Santa Fe, tel. 800/231–2222). **Faust's Transportation** (tel. 505/758–7359). **Texas, New Mexico & Oklahoma Coaches** (490 N. Valley Dr., Las Cruces, tel. 800/231–2222).

WITHIN SANTA FE

The city's bus system, Santa Fe Trails, covers six major routes: Agua Fria, Cerrillos, West Alameda, Southside, Eastside, and

Galisteo. A daily pass costs $1. Buses run about every 30 minutes on weekdays, every hour on weekends. Service begins at 6 AM and continues until 10 PM on weekdays and until 8 PM on Saturday. There is no bus service on Sunday.

➤ **SANTA FE BUS INFORMATION: Santa Fe Trails** (tel. 505/438–1464).

WITHIN TAOS

The town of Taos transit department's Chile Lines bus service has two lines. The Green Line circles around town while the Red Line runs between Taos Pueblo and Ranchos de Taos post office. Tickets are 50¢, all-day passes $1.

➤ **TAOS BUS INFORMATION: Chile Line** (tel. 505/751–4459).

Business Hours

Banks generally are open in Santa Fe on weekdays between 9 and 3 and on Saturday between 9 and noon. In Taos they are open on weekdays between 9 and 5, and in Albuquerque on weekdays between 9 and 4. Some branches are open between 10 and noon on Saturday. The main post offices are open on weekdays from 8 to 5 (from 9 to 5 in Taos) and on Saturday between 9 and noon. Banks generally are open in Santa Fe on weekdays between 9 and 3 and on Saturday between 9 and noon. In Taos they are open on weekdays between 9 and 5. The main post offices are open on weekdays from 8 to 5 (from 9 to 5 in Taos) and on Saturday between 9 and noon. Museums are generally open daily from 9 or 10 AM to 5 or 6 PM, although hours may vary from season to season. Many are closed on Monday, and some are open for extended hours on Friday evening. Most shops and galleries are open between 10 and 5 or 6, with limited hours on weekends.

Cameras & Photography

New Mexico's wildlife and rugged landscape are extremely photogenic. The striking red sandstone cliffs and soil of northern New Mexico make a terrific backdrop. It's best to take photographs in the early morning or late evening to take advantage of more subtle lighting and escape the glare of the bright sun.

➤ Photo Help: **Kodak Information Center** (tel. 800/242–2424). *Kodak Guide to Shooting Great Travel Pictures,* available in bookstores or from Fodor's Travel Publications (tel. 800/533–6478; $18 plus $5.50 shipping).

EQUIPMENT PRECAUTIONS

Always **keep your film and tape out of the sun.** Carry an extra supply of batteries, and **be prepared to turn on your camera or camcorder** to prove to security personnel that the device is real. Always **ask for hand inspection of film,** which becomes clouded after repeated exposure to airport X-ray machines, and **keep videotapes away from metal detectors.** In New Mexico, dust can be a problem. Keep cameras and video equipment in cases while not in use. Also, keep in mind that extreme heat can ruin film. Don't leave your equipment in a hot car or under direct sunlight.

Car Rental

A typical rate in Santa Fe is about $40 daily and $200 weekly for an economy car with air-conditioning, automatic transmission, and unlimited mileage. Tax on car rentals is 10.75% with an additional $2 per day surcharge.

➤ Major Agencies: **Alamo** (tel. 800/327–9633; 020/8759–6200 in the U.K.). **Avis** (tel. 800/331–1212; 800/879–2847 in Canada; 02/9353–9000 in Australia; 09/525–1982 in New Zealand). **Budget** (tel. 800/527–0700; 0144/227–6266 in the U.K.). **Dollar** (tel. 800/800–4000; 020/8897–0811 in the U.K., where it is known as Eurodollar; 02/9223–1444 in Australia). **Hertz** (tel. 800/654–3131; 800/263–0600 in Canada; 020/8897–2072 in the U.K.; 02/9669–2444 in Australia; 03/358–6777 in New Zealand). **National Car Rental** (tel. 800/227–7368).

CUTTING COSTS

To get the best deal, **book through a travel agent, who will shop around.** Also **price local car-rental companies,** although the service and maintenance may not be as good as those of a major player. Remember to ask about required deposits, cancellation penalties, and drop-off charges if you're planning to pick up the car in one city and leave it in another. If you're traveling during a holiday period, also make sure that a confirmed reservation guarantees you a car.

INSURANCE

When driving a rented car you are generally responsible for any damage to or loss of the vehicle as well as for any property damage or personal injury that you may cause. Before you rent see what coverage your personal auto-insurance policy and credit cards already provide.

For about $15 to $20 per day, rental companies sell protection, known as a collision- or loss-damage waiver (CDW or LDW), that eliminates your liability for damage to the car. In most states you don't need a CDW if you have personal auto insurance or other liability insurance. However, **make sure you have enough coverage to pay for the car.** If you do not have auto insurance or an umbrella policy that covers damage to third parties, purchasing liability insurance and a CDW or LDW is highly recommended.

REQUIREMENTS & RESTRICTIONS

In New Mexico you must be 21 to rent a car, and rates may be higher if you're under 25. You'll pay extra for child seats (about $3 per day), which are compulsory for children under five, and for additional drivers (about $2 per day). Non-U.S. residents will need a reservation voucher, a passport, a driver's license, and a travel policy that covers each driver, when picking up a car.

SURCHARGES

Before you pick up a car in one city and leave it in another, **ask about drop-off charges or one-way service fees,** which can be substantial. Note, too, that some rental agencies charge extra if you return the car before the time specified in your contract. To avoid a hefty refueling fee, **fill the tank just before you turn in the car,** but be aware that gas stations near the rental outlet may overcharge.

Car Travel

A car is a necessity when visiting Santa Fe and Taos as the cities have minimal public transportation. Interstate 25 passes east–west through Santa Fe, which is 58 mi northeast of Albuquerque. U.S. 84/285 runs north–south through the city. The Turquoise Trail is a scenic two-lane approach to Santa Fe from Albuquerque. The main route from Santa Fe to Taos is NM 68, which winds between the Rio Grande and red-rock cliffs before rising to a spectacular view of the plain and river gorge. You can also take the wooded High Road to Taos from Santa Fe.

Roads can be treacherously icy in the winter months; call **New Mexico Road Conditions** (tel. 800/432–4269) before heading out. The altitude in Taos will affect your car's performance, causing it to "gasp" because it's getting too much gas and not enough air. If a smooth ride matters, you can have your car tuned up for high-altitude driving.

PARKING

Parking in Santa Fe is difficult, but public and private lots can be found throughout the city. Parking meters are well monitored. There are parking garages near the Plaza on W. San Franscisco, between Sandoval and Galisteo, and on Water Street, between Don Gaspar and Shelby Street.

In Taos, metered parking areas are all over town; in peak seasons—summer and winter—traffic and parking can be a headache. There's a metered parking lot between Taos Plaza and Bent Street and a free lot on Kit Carson two blocks east of Paseo del Pueblo.

ROAD MAPS

The New Mexico Department of Tourism provides a detailed map of the state on request. GTR Mapping produces a topographical map of the state that depicts many backroads and recreational sites. The GTR maps are sold at convenience and grocery stores, bookstores, and department stores like Kmart and Wal-Mart.

➤ Maps: **New Mexico Department of Tourism** (tel. 505/827–7400 or 800/545–2070). **GTR Mapping** (tel. 719/275–8948).

RULES OF THE ROAD

The speed limit along the interstates in much of New Mexico is 70 or 75 mph; it's 65 to 70 on U.S. highways (55 in more populated areas). In most areas you can turn right at a red light provided you come to a full stop and check to see that the intersection is clear first. The use of seat belts in the front of the car is required by law in New Mexico. Always **strap children under age five into approved child-safety seats.** The state has an unusually high incidence of drunken driving–related accidents, and you might encounter sobriety checkpoints. The legal adult blood alcohol content (BAC) limit is .08.

Consumer Protection

Whenever shopping or buying travel services, **pay with a major credit card** so you can cancel payment or get reimbursed if there's a problem. If you're doing business with a particular company for the first time, **contact your local Better Business Bureau and the attorney general's offices** in your own state and the company's home state, as well. Have any complaints been filed? Finally, if you're buying a package or tour, always **consider travel insurance** that includes default coverage (☞ Insurance, *below*).

➤ BBBs: **Better Business Bureau**(2625 Pennsylvania NE, Suite 2050, Albuquerque, NM 87110, tel. 505/884–0500 or 800/873–2224 in NM, fax 505/346–0696, www.bbbnm.com). **Council of Better**

Business Bureaus (4200 Wilson Blvd., Suite 800, Arlington, VA 22203, tel. 703/276–0100, fax 703/525–8277, www.bbb.org).

Dining

New Mexico has some of the best Mexican food in the Southwest, and ingredients and style vary even within the state. Excellent barbecue and steaks also can be found throughout New Mexico. The restaurants we list are the cream of the crop in each price category.

CATEGORY	COST*
$$$$	over $30
$$$	$20–$30
$$	$10–$20
$	under $10

*per person for a three-course meal, excluding drinks, service, and sales tax (5.6%–7%)

RESERVATIONS & DRESS
Reservations are always a good idea: we mention them only when they're essential or not accepted. State-wide, many kitchens stop serving around 8 PM, so **don't arrive too late** if you're looking forward to a leisurely dinner. We mention dress only when men are required to wear a jacket or a jacket and tie. Even at nicer restaurants in Santa Fe and Taos, dress is usually casual.

Discounts & Deals

Be a smart shopper and **compare all your options** before making decisions. A plane ticket bought with a promotional coupon from travel clubs, coupon books, and direct-mail offers may not be cheaper than the least expensive fare from a discount ticket agency. And always keep in mind that what you get is just as important as what you save.

DISCOUNT RESERVATIONS

To save money, **look into discount reservations services** with toll-free numbers, which use their buying power to get a better price on hotels, airline tickets, even car rentals. When booking a room, always **call the hotel's local toll-free number** (if one is available) rather than the central reservations number—you'll often get a better price. Always ask about special packages or corporate rates.

➤ AIRLINE TICKETS: tel. **800/FLY-ASAP.**

➤ HOTEL ROOMS: **RMC Travel** (tel. 800/245-5738, www. rmcwebtravel.com). **Steigenberger Reservation Service** (tel. 800/223-5652, www.srs-worldhotels.com). **Turbotrip.com** (tel. 800/473-7829, www.turbotrip.com).

PACKAGE DEALS

Don't confuse packages and guided tours. When you buy a package, you travel on your own, just as though you had planned the trip yourself. Fly-drive packages, which combine airfare and car rental, are often a good deal.

Emergencies

For an ambulance, the fire department, or the police, dial 911.

➤ HOSPITALS: **Holy Cross Hospital** (630 Paseo del Pueblo Sur, Taos, tel. 505/758-8883). **St. Vincent Hospital, Medical Emergency Room** (455 St. Michael's Dr., Santa Fe, tel. 505/820-5250).

➤ PHARMACIES: **Taos Pharmacy** (Piñon Plaza, 622A Paseo del Pueblo Sur, Taos, tel. 505/758-3342). **Walgreens** (1096 S. St. Francis Dr., Santa Fe, tel. 505/982-9811).

Etiquette & Behavior

See Reservations and Pueblos *in* Introducing Santa Fe and Taos for information about proper etiquette when visiting Native American lands.

Gay & Lesbian Travel

Although Santa Fe doesn't have a highly visible gay community or a swinging gay nightlife, lesbians and gay men have long been a presence, and a short section of North Guadalupe Street is developing into a local hangout. The monthly *Out! Magazine* (no relation to the national magazine *Out*) provides coverage of New Mexico. A chapter in *Fodor's Gay Guide to the USA* covers Santa Fe, Taos, and Albuquerque.

➤ RESOURCES: **Fodor's Gay Guide to the USA,** available in bookstores or from Fodor's Travel Publications (tel. 800/533–6478; $20 plus $4 shipping). **Out! Magazine** (tel. 505/243–2540).

Guided Tours

FROM SANTA FE

Aboot About has been walking groups through the history, art, and architecture of Santa Fe for 20 years. Tours take about two hours. No reservations are required. Afoot in Santa Fe Walking Tours conducts a two-hour close-up look at the city. Gray Line Tours of Santa Fe operates guided outings to Taos, the Bandelier cliff dwellings, Los Alamos, and the Santa Clara pueblo. It also offers city tours and a minibus charter service. Santa Fe Detours conducts bus, river, rail, horseback, and walking tours and organizes rafting and ski packages. Storytellers and the Southwest surveys Santa Fe through its literary history. The two-hour literary walking tour explores the history, legends, characters, and authors of the region. Tours are by appointment only.

➤ TOUR OPERATORS: **Aboot About** (tel. 505/988–2774). **Afoot in Santa Fe Walking Tours** (211 Old Santa Fe Trail, tel. 505/983–3701). **Gray Line Tours of Santa Fe** (1330 Hickox St., tel. 505/983–9491). **Santa Fe Detours** (107 Washington Ave., outdoor booth Mar.–Oct.; 54½ San Francisco St., above Häagen-Dazs, tel. 505/983–6565 or 800/338–6877). **Storytellers and the Southwest** (tel. 505/989–4561).

FROM TAOS

Historic Taos Trolley Tours conducts two three-hour narrated tours of Taos daily, including stops at the San Francisco de Asís Church, Taos Pueblo, La Hacienda de los Martínez, and a Taos drum shop. Tours run from May to October. Taos Studio Tours offers individual or small group tours to galleries and artists' studios as well as excursions in and around town. All Aboard guide service conducts 1½-hr walking tours in town. Native Sons Adventures organizes biking, backpacking, rafting, snowmobiling, and horseback and wagon expeditions.

➤ TOUR OPERATORS: **Historic Taos Trolley Tours** (tel. 505/751–0366). **Taos Studio Tours** (tel. 505/776–9749). **All Aboard** (tel. 505/758–9368). **Native Sons Adventures** (715 Paseo del Pueblo Sur, tel. 505/758–9342 or 800/753–7559).

Holidays

Santa Fe and Taos are exceptional destinations at Christmastime. There's an excellent chance for snow to put you in the holiday mood, but usually not too much of it and at tolerable temperatures.

Major national holidays include New Year's Day (Jan. 1); Martin Luther King, Jr., Day (3rd Mon. in Jan.); Presidents' Day (3rd Mon. in Feb.); Memorial Day (last Mon. in May); Independence Day (July 4); Labor Day (1st Mon. in Sept.); Thanksgiving Day (4th Thurs. in Nov.); Christmas Eve and Christmas Day (Dec. 24 and 25); and New Year's Eve (Dec. 31).

Insurance

The most useful travel-insurance plan is a comprehensive policy that includes coverage for trip cancellation and interruption, default, trip delay, and medical expenses (with a waiver for preexisting conditions).

Without insurance you will lose all or most of your money if you cancel your trip, regardless of the reason. Default insurance covers you if your tour operator, airline, or cruise line goes out of business. Trip-delay covers expenses that arise because of bad weather or mechanical delays. Study the fine print when comparing policies.

Always **buy travel policies directly from the insurance company**; if you buy them from a cruise line, airline, or tour operator that goes out of business you probably will not be covered for the agency or operator's default, a major risk. Before making any purchase, **review your existing health and home-owner's policies** to find what they cover away from home.

➤ TRAVEL INSURERS: In the U.S.: **Access America** (6600 W. Broad St., Richmond, VA 23230, tel. 804/285-3300 or 800/284-8300, fax 804/673-1583, www.previewtravel.com), **Travel Guard International** (1145 Clark St., Stevens Point, WI 54481, tel. 715/345-0505 or 800/826-1300, fax 800/955-8785, www.noelgroup.com).

Lodging

The lodgings we list are the cream of the crop in each price category. We always list the facilities that are available—but we don't specify whether they cost extra: when pricing accommodations, always ask what's included and what costs extra. Accommodations in New Mexico include inexpensive chain hotels, many bed-and-breakfasts, small alpine lodges near the primary ski resorts, and low-budget motels. Rates are highest during the peak tourist months of July and August and during Christmas and winter ski season. Off-season rates, which fluctuate, tend to be 20% lower than peak rates, and reservations are easier to obtain at this time. You can book rooms (and rental cars and outdoor and other activities) by calling New Mexico Central Reservations.

CATEGORY	COST*
$$$$	over $150
$$$	$100–$150
$$	$65–$100
$	under $65

All prices are for a standard double room, excluding tax (5.6%–7%), in peak season.

➤ RESERVATIONS: **New Mexico Central Reservations** (tel. 800/466–7829).

B&BS

B&Bs in New Mexico run the gamut from rooms in locals' homes to grandly restored adobe or Victorian homes. Rates in Santa Fe and Taos tend to be high.

➤ RESERVATION SERVICES: **Bed and Breakfast of New Mexico** (tel. 505/982–3332). **New Mexico Bed and Breakfast Association** (tel. 505/766–5380 or 800/661–6649).

HOTELS

The Fourth of July weekend can pack hotel rooms towns such as Taos, so make sure you have reservations in advance.

➤ TOLL-FREE NUMBERS: **Baymont Inns** (tel. 800/428–3438, www.baymontinns.com). **Best Western** (tel. 800/528–1234, www.bestwestern.com). **Choice** (tel. 800/221–2222, www. hotelchoice.com). **Clarion** (tel. 800/252–7466, www. choicehotels.com). **Colony** (tel. 800/777–1700. www.colony.com). **Comfort** (tel. 800/228–5150, www.comfortinn.com). **Days Inn** (tel. 800/325–2525, www.daysinn.com). **Doubletree and Red Lion Hotels** (tel. 800/222–8733, www.doubletree.com). **Embassy Suites** (tel. 800/362–2779, www.embassysuites.com). **Fairfield Inn** (tel. 800/228–2800, www.marriott.com). **Four Seasons** (tel. 800/332–3442, www.fourseasons.com). **Hilton** (tel. 800/445–8667, www.hiltons.com). **Holiday Inn** (tel. 800/465–4329, www.basshotels.com). **Howard Johnson** (tel. 800/654–4656, www.hojo.com). **Hyatt Hotels & Resorts** (tel. 800/233–1234, www.hyatt.com). **La Quinta** (tel. 800/531–5900, www.laquinta.com). **Marriott** (tel. 800/228–9290, www.marriott.com). **Quality Inn** (tel. 800/228–5151, www.qualityinn.com). **Radisson** (tel. 800/333–3333, www.radisson.com). **Ramada** (tel. 800/228–2828. www.ramada.com), **Sheraton** (tel. 800/325–3535, www.sheraton.com). **Sleep Inn** (tel. 800/753–3746, www.sleepinn.com). **Westin Hotels & Resorts** (tel. 800/228–3000, www.westin.com). **Wyndham Hotels & Resorts** (tel. 800/822–4200, www.wyndham.com).

MOTELS

➤ **TOLL-FREE NUMBERS: Econo Lodge** (tel. 800/553–2666). **Hampton Inn** (tel. 800/426–7866). **La Quinta** (tel. 800/531–5900). **Motel 6** (tel. 800/466–8356). **Rodeway** (tel. 800/228–2000). **Super 8** (tel. 800/848–8888).

Money Matters

Santa Fe is by far New Mexico's priciest city: meals, gasoline, and motel rates are all significantly higher in the state's capital. Taos, too, can be a little expensive because it's such a popular tourist destination, but you have more choices for economizing there than in Santa Fe. Prices throughout this guide are given for adults. Substantially reduced fees are almost always available for children, students, and senior citizens.

ATMS

Look for ATMs in larger communities, since isolated rural areas are not as widely served. ATMs are available in banks, bank branches, chain grocery stores, and shopping malls.

CREDIT CARDS

Throughout this guide, the following abbreviations are used: **AE,** American Express; **D,** Discover; **DC,** Diners Club; **MC,** MasterCard; and **V,** Visa.

➤ **REPORTING LOST CARDS: American Express** (tel. 800/300–8765). **Diners Club** (tel. 800/234–6377). **DiscoverCard** (tel. 800/347–

2683). **MasterCard** (tel. 800/826–2181). **Visa** (tel. 800/336–8472).

Packing

Typical of the Southwest, temperatures can vary considerably from sunup to sundown. You should **pack for warm days and chilly nights.** In winter pack warm clothes—coats, parkas, and whatever else your body's thermostat dictates. Sweaters and jackets are also needed in summer, because though days are warm, nights at the higher altitudes can be extremely chilly. And **bring comfortable shoes;** you're likely to be doing a lot of walking.

New Mexico is one of the most informal and laid-back areas of the country, which for many is much a part of its appeal. Probably no more than three or four restaurants in the entire state enforce a dress code, even for dinner, though men are likely to feel more comfortable wearing a jacket in the major hotel dining rooms, and anyone wearing tennis shoes may receive a look of stern disapproval from the maître d'.

In your carry-on luggage, **pack an extra pair of eyeglasses or contact lenses** and **enough of any medication you take** to last the entire trip. You may also ask your doctor to write a spare prescription using the drug's generic name, since brand names may vary from country to country. In luggage to be checked, **never pack prescription drugs or valuables.** To avoid customs delays, carry medications in their original packaging. And don't forget to carry with you the addresses of offices that handle refunds of lost traveler's checks. If you are traveling with a wine opener, pocketknife, or any other kind of knife, or toy weapons, **pack them in check-in luggage.** These are considered potential weapons and are not permitted as carry-on items.

CHECKING LUGGAGE

How many carry-on bags you can bring with you is up to the airline. Most allow two, but some allow only one (including

United, a major carrier in New Mexico), so make sure that everything you carry aboard will fit under your seat or in the overhead bin, and get to the gate early. Note that if you have a seat at the back of the plane, you'll probably board first, while the overhead bins are still empty.

Airline liability for baggage is limited to $1,250 per person on flights within the United States. On international flights it amounts to $9.07 per pound or $20 per kilogram for checked baggage (roughly $640 per 70-pound bag) and $400 per passenger for unchecked baggage. You can buy additional coverage at check-in for about $10 per $1,000 of coverage, but it excludes a rather extensive list of items, shown on your airline ticket.

Before departure, **itemize your bags' contents** and their worth, and label the bags with your name, address, and phone number. (If you use your home address, cover it so potential thieves can't see it readily.) Inside each bag, **pack a copy of your itinerary.** At check-in, **make sure that each bag is correctly tagged** with the destination airport's three-letter code. If your bags arrive damaged or fail to arrive at all, file a written report with the airline before leaving the airport. Attendants at Albuquerque's airport match your luggage's baggage claim ticket to the number placed on your boarding pass envelope, **so have the envelope handy as you exit the baggage claim area.**

Taxis

Capital City Cab Company controls all the cabs in Santa Fe. The taxis aren't metered; you pay a flat fee determined by the distance you're traveling. There are no cab stands; you must phone to arrange a ride. Trips within the city cost between $4 and $7.

Taxi service in Taos is sparse. However, Faust's Transportation, based in nearby El Prado, has a fleet of radio-dispatched cabs.

➤ Taxi Companies: **Capital City Cab Company** (tel. 505/438–
0000). **Faust's Transportation** (tel. 505/758–3410 or 505/758–
7359).

Time

New Mexico observes Mountain Standard Time, switching over
with most of the rest of the country to Daylight Saving Time in
the spring through fall. In New Mexico, you'll be two hours
behind New York and one hour ahead of Arizona and California.

Tours & Packages

Because everything is prearranged on a prepackaged tour or
independent vacation, you'll spend less time planning—and
often get it all at a good price.

BOOKING WITH AN AGENT

Travel agents are excellent resources. But it's a good idea to collect
brochures from several agencies, as some agents' suggestions
may be influenced by relationships with tour and package firms
that reward them for volume sales. If you have a special interest,
find an agent with expertise in that area; ASTA (☞ Travel
Agencies, *below*) has a database of specialists worldwide.

Make sure your travel agent knows the accommodations and
other services of the place being recommended. Ask about the
hotel's location, room size, beds, and whether it has a pool,
room service, or programs for children, if you care about these.
Has your agent been there in person or sent others whom you
can contact?

Do some homework on your own, too: local tourism boards can
provide information about lesser-known and small-niche
operators, some of which may sell only direct.

BUYER BEWARE

Each year consumers are stranded or lose their money when
tour operators—even large ones with excellent reputations—go

out of business. So **check out the operator.** Ask several travel agents about its reputation, and try to **book with a company that has a consumer-protection program.** (Look for information in the company's brochure.) In the United States, members of the National Tour Association and the United States Tour Operators Association are required to set aside funds to cover your payments and travel arrangements in the event that the company defaults. It's also a good idea to choose a company that participates in the American Society of Travel Agents' Tour Operator Program (TOP); ASTA will act as mediator in any disputes between you and your tour operator.

Remember that the more your package or tour includes the better you can predict the ultimate cost of your vacation. Make sure you know exactly what is covered, and **beware of hidden costs.** Are taxes, tips, and transfers included? Entertainment and excursions? These can add up.

➤ TOUR-OPERATOR RECOMMENDATIONS: **American Society of Travel Agents** (☞ Travel Agencies, *below*). **National Tour Association** (NTA; 546 E. Main St., Lexington, KY 40508, tel. 606/226–4444 or 800/682–8886, www.ntaonline.com). **United States Tour Operators Association** (USTOA; 342 Madison Ave., Suite 1522, New York, NY 10173, tel. 212/599–6599 or 800/468–7862, fax 212/599–6744, www.ustoa.com).

Train Travel

Amtrak operates the *Southwest Chief* between Chicago and Los Angeles. The train stops in Lamy, 18 mi south of Santa Fe.

➤ TRAIN INFORMATION: **Amtrak** (tel. 800/872–7245).

Transportation around New Mexico

A tour bus or car is the best way to take in the entire state. Public transportation options do exist in metropolitan areas, but they are not very convenient. Don't expect to find easy transportation for rural excursions. Bus or van service exists for virtually every community on the map, but be prepared for frequent stops for pickups along rural routes.

Travel Agencies

A good travel agent puts your needs first. Look for an agency that has been in business at least five years, emphasizes customer service, and has someone on staff who specializes in your destination. In addition, **make sure the agency belongs to a professional trade organization.** The American Society of Travel Agents (ASTA), with 27,000 agents in some 170 countries, is the largest and most influential in the field. Operating under the motto "Integrity in Travel," it maintains and enforces a strict code of ethics and will step in to help mediate any agent-client disputes if necessary. ASTA also maintains a Web site that includes a directory of agents. If a travel agency is also acting as your tour operator, *see* Buyer Beware *in* Tours & Packages, *above.*

➤ LOCAL AGENT REFERRALS: **American Society of Travel Agents** (ASTA; tel. 800/965–2782 24-hr hot line, fax 703/684–8319, www.astanet.com). **Association of British Travel Agents** (68–71 Newman St., London W1P 4AH, tel. 020/7637–2444, fax 020/7637–0713, www.abtanet.com). **Association of Canadian Travel Agents** (1729 Bank St., Suite 201, Ottawa, Ontario K1V 7Z5, tel. 613/237–3657, fax 613/521–0805).

Visitor Information

For general information before you go, contact the city and state tourism bureaus. For information about Native American attractions, call or visit the Indian Pueblo Cultural Center.

➤ CITY INFORMATION: **Santa Fe Convention and Visitors Bureau** (Box 909, Santa Fe 87504, tel. 505/984–6760 or 800/777–2489, fax 505/984–6679. www.santafe.org). **Taos County Chamber of Commerce** (Drawer I, Taos 87571, tel. 505/758–3873 or 800/732–8267, fax 505/758–3872. www.taoschamber.com).

➤ **STATEWIDE INFORMATION: New Mexico Department of Tourism** (491 Old Santa Fe Trail, Santa Fe 87503, tel. 505/827–7400 or 800/545–2070, fax 505/827–7402. www.newmexico.org).

➤ **NATIVE ATTRACTIONS: Indian Pueblo Cultural Center** (2401 12th St. NW, Albuquerque 87102, tel. 505/843–7270; 800/766–4405 outside NM, fax 505/842–6959).

Web Sites

Do check out the World Wide Web when you're planning your trip. You'll find everything from current weather forecasts to virtual tours of famous cities. Fodor's Web site, www.fodors. com, is a great place to start your on-line travels.

Official Web sites of tourism offices are listed under Visitor Information (☞ *above*).

When to Go

The majority of major events—including the Santa Fe Opera, Chamber Music Festival, and Indian and Spanish markets—are geared to the traditionally heavy tourist season of July and August. The Santa Fe Fiesta is held in September.

The relatively cool climates of Santa Fe and Taos are a lure in summer, as is the skiing in winter. Christmas is a wonderful time to be in New Mexico because of Native American ceremonies as well as the Hispanic religious folk plays, special foods, and musical events. Hotel rates are generally highest during the peak summer season but fluctuate less than those in most major resort areas. If you plan to come in summer, **be sure to make reservations in advance for July and August.** You can avoid most of the tourist crowds by coming during spring or fall.

➤ **FORECASTS: Weather Channel Connection** (tel. 900/932–8437), 95¢ per minute from a Touch-Tone phone.

The following are average daily maximum and minimum temperatures for Santa Fe.

SANTA FE

Jan.	39F	4C	May	68F	20C	Sept.	73F	23C
	19	-7		42	6		48	9
Feb.	42F	6C	June	78F	26C	Oct.	62F	17C
	23	-5		51	11		37	3
Mar.	51F	11C	July	80F	27C	Nov.	50F	10C
	28	-2		57	14		28	-2
Apr.	59F	15C	Aug.	78F	26C	Dec.	39F	4C
	35	2		55	13		19	-7

GLOSSARY

Perhaps more than any other region in the United States, New Mexico has its own distinctive cuisine heavily influenced by Native American, Spanish-colonial, Mexican, and American frontier traditions.

As befits a land occupied—in several senses of the word in some cases—by so many diverse peoples, the use of accents on place and other names is a tricky matter. For some people, among them many Hispanic residents, accents are a matter of identification and pride—Río Grande, for instance, represents more clearly the linguistic origins of the current name of the river that runs so grandly through the state. On the other hand, though including the accent for Picurís Pueblo or Jémez Pueblo might be linguistically accurate, it's also a reminder to a Pueblo Native American of his or her nation's conquest by the Spanish. ("I couldn't care less whether you use accents or not—I don't," said a woman at the governor's office of Jemez Pueblo when asked whether having an accent above the first "e" in the pueblo's name would be more accurate.)

In general in this book we've applied accents when they're part of an official place or other name. Signs for and official documents of Española, for instance, tend to have a tilde above the "n" in the city's name. On the other hand, though the names of Capulin Volcano and the city of Raton are sometimes written Capulín Volcano and Ratón, we have not employed the accents because New Mexican residents rarely do. A generally workable solution, this strategy does leads to some apparent inconsistencies (Picurís Pueblo; Jemez Pueblo), an illustration of the conflicting cultural sentiments still at play within New Mexico.

MENU GUIDE

Aguacate: Spanish for avocado, the key ingredient of guacamole

Albóndigas: Meatballs, usually cooked with rice in a meat broth

Bolsa del pobre: A seafood and vegetable dish; a specialty from Colima

Burrito: A warm flour tortilla wrapped around meat, beans, and vegetables, and smothered in chile and cheese

Carne adovada: Red chile-marinated pork

Chalupa: A corn tortilla deep-fried in the shape of a bowl, filled with pinto beans (sometimes meat), and topped with cheese, guacamole, sour cream, lettuce, tomatoes, and salsa

Chile relleno: A large green chile pepper peeled, stuffed with cheese or a special mixture of spicy ingredients, dipped in batter, and fried

Chiles: New Mexico's infamous hot peppers, which come in an endless variety of sizes and in various degrees of hotness, from the thumb-size jalapeño to the smaller and often hotter serrano; they can be canned or fresh, dried or cut up into salsa

Chimichanga: The same as a burrito (☞ above), only deep-fried and topped with a dab of sour cream or salsa

Chipotle: A dried smoked jalepeño with a smoky, almost sweet, chocolatey flavor

Chorizo: Well-spiced Spanish sausage, made with pork and red chiles

Enchilada: A rolled or flat corn tortilla filled with meat, chicken, seafood, or cheese, an enchilada is covered with chile and baked. The ultimate enchilada is made with blue Indian corn tortillas. New Mexicans order them flat, sometimes topped with a fried egg.

Fajitas: Grilled beef, chicken, or fish with peppers and onions, served with tortillas; traditionally known as arracheras

Flauta: A tortilla filled with cheese or meat, rolled into a flutelike shape (*flauta* means flute) and lightly fried

Frijoles refritos: Refried beans, often seasoned with lard or cheese

Guacamole: Mashed avocado, mixed with tomatoes, garlic, onions, lemon juice, and chiles, used as a dip, a side dish, a topping, or an additional ingredient

Huevos rancheros: New Mexico's answer to eggs Benedict— eggs doused with chile and sometimes melted cheese, served on top of a corn tortilla (they're good accompanied by chorizo)

Pan de cazón: Grilled shark with black beans and red onions on a tortilla; a specialty from Campeche

Posole: Resembling popcorn soup, this is a sublime marriage of lime, hominy, pork, chile, garlic, and spices

Quesadilla: A folded flour tortilla filled with cheese and meat or vegetables, and warmed or lightly fried so the cheese melts

Queso: Cheese; an ingredient in many Mexican and Southwestern recipes

Ristra: String of dried red chile peppers, often used as decoration

Sopaipilla: Puffy deep-fried bread, served with honey

Taco: A corn or flour tortilla baked or fried and made into a shell that's then stuffed with vegetables or spicy meat and garnished with shredded lettuce, chopped tomatoes, onions, and grated cheese

Tacos al carbón: Shredded pork cooked in a mole sauce and folded into corn tortillas

Tamale: Ground corn made into a dough and filled with finely ground pork and red chiles, then steamed in a corn husk

Tortilla: A thin pancake made of corn or wheat flour, a tortilla is used as bread, as an edible "spoon," and as a container for other foods. Locals place butter in the center of a hot tortilla, roll it up, and eat it as a scroll.

Trucha en terra-cotta: Fresh trout wrapped in corn husks and baked in clay

Verde: Spanish for "green," as in chile verde (a green chile sauce)

INDEX

FODOR'S POCKET SANTA FE & TAOS

EDITORS: Christina Knight, Sharron S. Wood

EDITORIAL CONTRIBUTORS: Jeanie Puleston Fleming, Marilyn Haddrill, Kathleen McCloud

EDITORIAL PRODUCTION: Marina Padakis

MAPS: David Lindroth, *cartographer;* Bob Blake and Rebecca Baer, *map editors*

DESIGN: Fabrizio La Rocca, *creative director;* Tigist Getachew, *art director;* Melanie Marin, *photo editor*

PRODUCTION/MANUFACTURING: Angela L. McLean

COVER PHOTOGRAPH: Buddy Mays/ Corbis

COPYRIGHT

IMPORTANT TIP

Although all prices, opening times, and other details in this book are based on information supplied to us at press time, changes occur all the time in the travel world, and Fodor's cannot accept responsibility for facts that become outdated or for inadvertent errors or omissions. So **always confirm information when it matters,** especially if you're making a detour to visit a specific place.

SPECIAL SALES